GREAT AMERICAN
SCENIC RAILROADS

GREAT AMERICAN SCENIC RAILROADS

MICHAEL SWIFT

CHARTWELL
BOOKS, INC.

This edition published in 2011 by

CHARTWELL BOOKS, INC.
A Division of
BOOK SALES, INC.
276 Fifth Avenue Suite 206
New York, New York 10001

ISBN 13: 978-0-7858-2853-2

Editor: Don Gulbrandsen
Design: Mark Tennent

Printed and bound in China
Reprinted 2012

Page 1: A gold star decorate the bright red hub of a
locomotive wheel at the State Railroad Museum in
Sacramento, California. *© Stephanie Maze/CORBIS*

Page 2/3: Durango & Silverton No. 481 is one of four
members of the "K-36" class to be based on the Colorado
line. *Brian Solomon*

Right: The Cumbres & Toltec is one of a number of scenic
railroads based on the narrow-gauge Denver & Rio Grande.
The line is host to five members of the "K-36" class dating
from 1925, including the 489 pictured here. *Brian Solomon*

Contents

Preface

Over the past 60 years, effectively since the end of World war II, there has been a revolution in society. People have acquired more leisure time and greater disposable incomes on the one hand and, on the other, many of the traditional industries that once formed the bedrock of the local economy have disappeared. Logging, for example, which was an essential part of the country's industrial base in places like California and West Virginia, has been significantly reduced over the years as forests have been exhausted and as new materials have replaced lumber in other trades.

One consequence of the changing economic pattern has been the gradual elimination of many of the country's secondary and minor railroad routes. Many of these had long since lost their passenger services, a reflection of the increased use of the automobile and the freedom associated with an automobile-owning society. However, the increased level of leisure—combined with types of lifestyle that were gradually disappearing—brought an increasing awareness that it might be possible to save something from the past to educate and entertain the present and future. The growth of the preservation industry—in many areas, not just rail—since 1945 that has been one of the most striking social revolutions over the past decades. Moreover, it is a revolution that continues to grow as new projects continue to appear and as older ones continue to expand. It is one of the paradoxes of modern society that, while more leisure time becomes available and as people live longer, so more and more get involved as volunteers doing work which one or two generations ago, would have been considered hard labor.

This book does not pretend to be a comprehensive account of each of the scenic railroads in the United States; rather it provides a potted history of many of the most

significant. Many are steam-operated but others, traversing some of the most stunning scenery that the country can offer, are diesel-operated. There are lines in most parts of the country and many offer a wide range of themed special or dining services. In an era when we should all be increasingly conscious of our impact on the environment, these scenic railroads have much to offer in allowing access to the countryside without destroying it.

The compilation of this book would not have been possible without the assistance of a number of individuals and bodies. In particular, the author would like to thank Derek Huntriss, Jim Livesey, Gavin Morrison, Brian Solomon, and John Vaughan for photographs from their own collections, and Katie Johnston from Corbis. Also of considerable help was the Online Transport Archive, a charity dedicated to the preservation of photographic collections covering transport and allied subjects.

Left: Built by Baldwin in 1912, EBT No 14 is pictured at Rockhill Furnace on 3 September 1961. *Harry Luff Collection/© Online Transport Archive*

Below: The world's first preserved standard-gauge railroad was the Strasburg Railroad in Pennsylvania. *H. Bongaardt*

Pages 8–9: GWR 2-10-0 No. 90—built by Baldwin in 1924—pictured at Goff's on the Strasburg Railroad, Pennsylvania, on August 23, 1973. *M. Randall*

Railroad Preservation

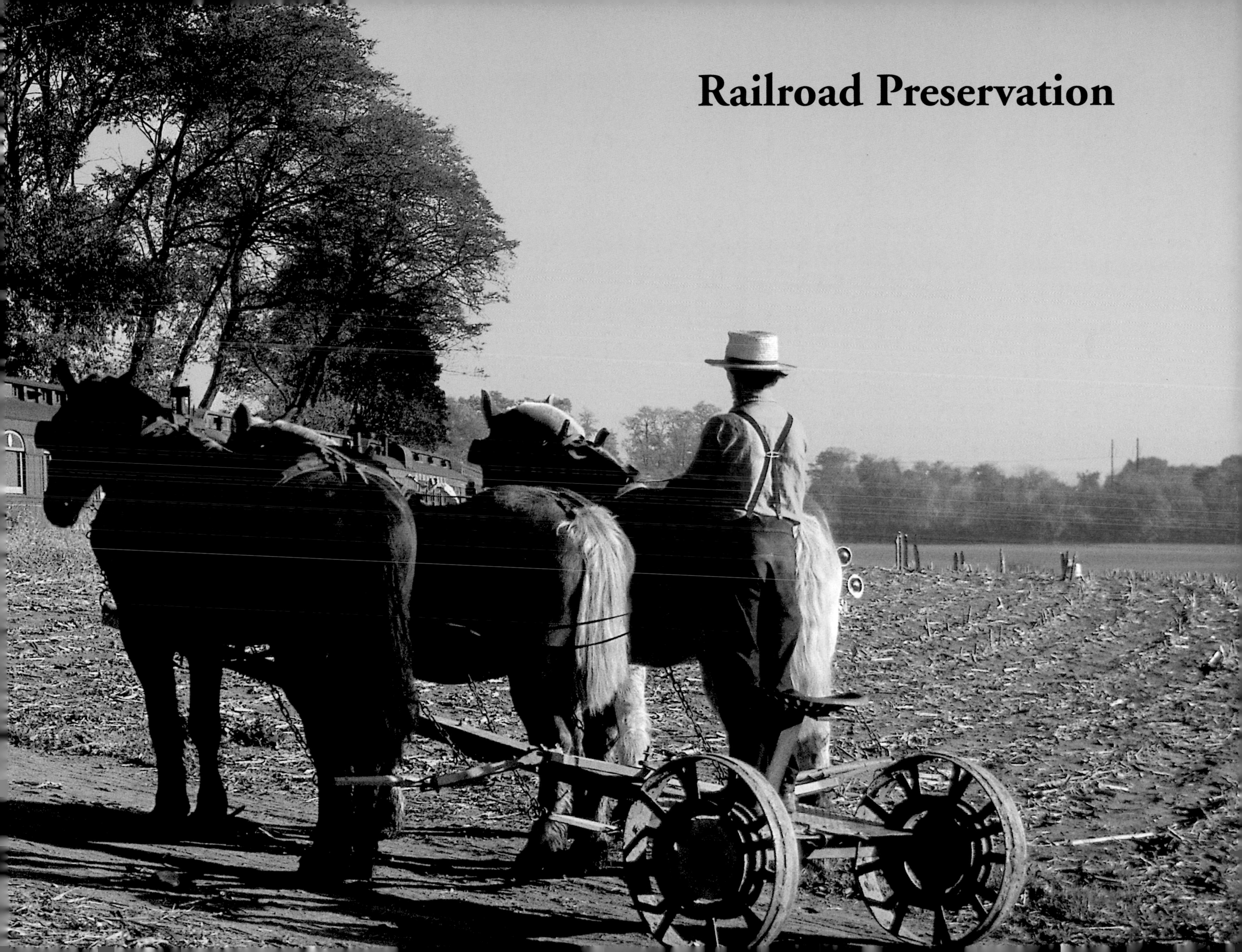

Railroad Preservation

Almost from the dawn of the railway age promoters realized that there was considerable commercial potential in the construction of lines specifically for tourists to be able to gain access to potentially attractive sites. In 1869 the Mount Washington cog railway opened; other examples of tourist-oriented routes included the Grand Canyon Railroad of the Santa Fe and the Georgetown Loop. However, just as the major railroads suffered from the rise of the internal combustion engine, so too did many of these pioneering tourist railways and—with exceptions (such as the Mount Washington line)—the majority fell by the wayside. This was not, necessarily, the end of the story as many of these lines have been resurrected in whole or in part—ironically, in many cases, as a means of reducing the pressure on tourist sites caused by road traffic. A notable example of this is the Grand Canyon line, which originally closed in 1968 but which reopened in 1991.

The first standard-gauge preserved line in the world was the Strasburg Railroad in Pennsylvania. The second oldest railway to receive a charter in the world—it obtained its charter on June 9, 1832; the Ffestiniog Railway in Wales beat it by a fortnight—the Strasburg Railroad provided a link ultimately between Strasburg and the main New York–Chicago line at Leaman Place. Freight only from 1920, the line was to close completely in 1958; however, having been purchased by Henry K. Long it reopened the following year and has now been carrying passengers as a tourist line for almost half a century. When the 4.5-mile long line was originally reopened, it was initially as a freight line, with a limited passenger service, but while revenue on freight was below expectations, that on the passenger side was encouraging enough to suggest that the company concentrate on this aspect. Where the Strasburg blazed a trail, other lines

Above: The Mount Washington Cog Railway has been in operation for almost 140 years. Its most recent locomotive is No 10. *Kroflite,* seen here, which was built in 1972. The locomotive was built in the railroad's own workshops. *Harry Luff Collection/© Online Transport Archive*

Right: The Cumbres & Toltec Scenic Railroad is one of a number of railroads that offer tourist services over the narrow gauge track of the erstwhile Denver & Rio Grande Railroad. *Harry Luff Collection/© Online Transport Archive*

both in the United States and throughout the world have followed.

In many respects the Strasburg Railroad's preservation is very typical of North American preservation. Unlike Europe, where many preservation schemes were not developed from any particular commercial aspiration but from a desire to preserve something that was in danger of being lost, much of preservation in the U.S. is more oriented toward the commercial tourist market. While there are the more conventional museums—such as the Baltimore & Ohio Railroad Museum and the Smithsonian—these are atypical.

While most European countries have state-sponsored national railroad museums covering the entire country's railroad history—such as Britain's National Railway Museum in York—there is nothing directly comparable in the U.S., although individual states may have such an institution. Moreover, while the majority of preserved lines in Europe are staffed almost exclusively with volunteers with relatively few paid staff, in the U.S. the reverse is true.

As part of the tourist industry there is an undoubted element of showbusiness in many of the U.S. "preserved" lines. A notable example of this is the three-mile long Tweetsie

Right: California Western Railroad No. 45 awaits departure from Fort Bragg during the summer of 1980. *Harry Luff Collection/© Online Transport Archive*

Below: In the fall of 1981, Durango & Silverton "K-36" No. 481 heads an excursion along the line. *Jim Livesey*

Left: Ex-Union Pacific "Big Boy" No. 4012, built by Alco in 1941, preserved at Steamtown. *Harry Luff Collection/© Online Transport Archive*

Above: Ex-Baltimore & Ohio No. 5300, dating from 1927, stands outside the B&O Museum in Baltimore on display. *Harry Luff Collection/© Online Transport Archive*

Page 16–17: No. 734 is the only steam locomotive on the Western Maryland's roster and the line uses diesel traction for its freight services and for a number of passenger duties as well. *Derek Huntriss*

Railroad, near Blowing Rock, North Carolina. Closer in concept to a theme park, trains are held up by "bandits" and attacked by "Indians" before returning passengers to Tweetsie Town where a typical railroad town of the end of the 19th century has been faithfully reconstructed.

There are more conservative examples of preserved railways of a style recognizable to those involved in preservation in Europe. One example of this is Valley Railroad in Connecticut. Largely staffed by volunteers of the Connecticut Valley Railroad Museum, the line operates for five miles between Essex and Chester.

Moreover, as the operation of these types of tourist service is a purely commercial undertaking, there is always the possibility that the promoter may collapse financially and there have been a number of lines that have had excursion trains where these services have been through the hands of a number of franchisees. Increasingly, however, non-profit organizations are taking over a number of the most important lines and operations. These bodies, backed often by the local population or by local or state authorities, are much more akin to the preservation societies that operate throughout much of Europe.

While examples of many of the most important designs of steam locomotive have survived—including no fewer than eight of the Union Pacific "Big Boys" of 1941—there are also countless examples of classic designs that have not survived. Among the many losses are examples of the streamlined "J3" class "Hudsons" of the New York Central and the same company's iconic "Niagara" class 4-8-4s of 1945–46. Although efforts were made to try and preserve at least one example of the former, prevailing attitudes in the period were such that the efforts failed. Two members of the Smithsonian Institute approached the NYC with a view to trying to acquire an example in the mid-1950s, when the last of the type was being withdrawn only to have their request rejected by the company's president, S. J. Pearlman; like many of his contemporaries, Pearlman believed that steam was obsolescent and that, on withdrawal, the locomotives should be consigned to the scrapyard.

The strength of the preservation movement is that it is a nationwide phenomenon. There are examples of museums from

Left: Ex-Union Pacific Challenger 4-6-6-4 No. 3985 undergoes maintenance at the roundhouse at Cheyenne, Wyoming, in November 1979. *P. J. Howard*

Right: As many U.S. scenic railroads are commercial, they face the same financial pressures as other businesses and many do not survive. One such casualty was the Valley Forge Scenic Railroad in Pennsylvania, which operated only between 1968 and 1969. Ex- Gulf, Mobile & Northern 4-6-2 No. 425 is pictured at Kimberton, Pennsylvania, on the Valley Forge Scenic Railroad during the line's short life. *H. Bongaardt*

across the country, from the Baltimore & Ohio Museum in Baltimore across to the California State Railroad Museum. There are also countless preserved lines, both standard and narrow gauge, offering tourists the opportunity of sampling railway travel as it existed in the past. But preservation is more than simply locomotives and rolling stock; it also involves the conservation of historical artefacts—from tickets to timetables and from signals to stationery. These are not the most glamorous parts of the nation's railway heritage, but without their conservation future generations will not be able to appreciate fully the rich heritage of United States railroading history.

Moreover, it's a history that moves forward day by day; just as the steam locomotive was deemed outmoded in the 1950s, so more recent locomotives and rolling stock are also gradually becoming obsolescent. The original EMD diesels are now as much a part of history as the steam locomotives they were destined to replace and many examples of these types of rolling stock are also finding their way into museum collections.

It's not just the preservationists that have realized that money can be made from the running of special trains. Increasingly, the commercial companies themselves have realized that money can be made from the running of special trains aimed at tourists. A notable example of this is the Arcade & Attica Railroad in New York State; the railroad initially withdrew all passenger services in 1951 but reintroduced a steam service in 1962. Such has been the success of the service over the 7.5 miles between Arcade and Curriers that the company now runs a regular tourist service each summer. Another main line company to have operated steam specials was the Southern Railway, which employed three steam locomotives for a number of years. Two of these were 2-8-0s built originally for the company but sold when steam was

Left: Now part of the Colorado Railroad Museum collection, 3ft 0in (914mm gauge) three-truck Shay No. 14 was constructed for the Colorado Central railroad and ran between Blackhawk and Central City—a four-mile section that including two switchbacks to cover the actual distance of one mile between the two places. *P. J. Howard*

withdrawn before being reacquired for these services. the third was a further 2-8-0, this time loaned by the Tennessee Valley Railroad Museum. With the merger of the Southern with the Norfolk & Western in 1982, the newly enlarged company expanded its steam operations, restoring the classic Norfolk & Western "J" class 4-8-4 No. 611 to service.

In a sense, with the realization by the main railroad companies that money can be made from these services, preservation has come full circle. Initially designed to try and secure historical items that were considered life-expired and uncommercial from the major companies, the major companies have now come to realize that such assets can be used to bring in additional revenue.

Left: Apart from museums and scenic lines, there are a number of locomotives preserved in other locations. One such example is ex-Santa Fe No. 3759, built by the Baldwin Locomotive Works in 1928, and presented to Kingman, Arizona, in 1957. It is listed on the National Register of Historic Places and stands along with a red caboose on a short piece of track. It is pictured here on April 12, 1990. *Gavin Morrison*

Right: "K-36" No. 489 climbs towards Cumbres Summit on the Cumbres & Toltec Scenic Railroad in Colorado. *Derek Huntriss*

The Railroads

Abilene & Smoky Valley Railroad

Based in Abilene, Kansas, the not-for-profit A&SVR provides heritage services between May and October. Founded in 1993 and located at the historic 1887 Rock Island Depot, the railroad operates for five miles between Abilene and Enterprise, Kansas, along the Smoky Hill River Valley with the return journey taking some 90 minutes. Services are currently hauled by a 1945 Alco S-1 diesel-electric locomotive although a steam locomotive, 1919 Baldwin-built Pacific No. 3415 of the Santa Fe, is currently under restoration. Beyond Enterprise, a railbus operates for a further 12 miles to Woodbine over a recently opened extension.

Adirondack Scenic Railroad

Based at Thendara, New York, the Adirondack Scenic Railroad operates two sections of standard gauge line—from Uttica to Thendara and from Lake Placid to Saranac Lake—although its long-term plan is to reconnect the two sections. The two sections were part of a line constructed in 1892 which became part, eventually, of the New York Central Railroad and, in the 1950s, of Penn Central. In 1961 part of the line, from Lake Clear Junction to Malone, was abandoned and passenger services from Uttica to Lake Placid were withdrawn four years later. Freight traffic, however, continued until 1972, when Penn Central sought permission to abandon the 118-mile long route. This was approved by the Public Service Commission. This might have been the end of the story but in 1975 the state acquired the derelict line as a "transportation asset," and in 1979 and 1980, limited passenger services were provided by the Adirondack Railway Corporation. The contract was terminated in February 1981 but it was not until the early 1990s, after a legal dispute, that the possibility of tourist services again surfaced. In 1992 limited services were introduced over the Uttica-Thendara section, and the success of these encouraged the state governor, George E. Pataki, to see the development of the

entire 118-mile line for leisure activities. On the Thendara section, there are services to Uttica and shorter trips to the north, to Carter Station, and to the south, to Otter Lake, which offer a 20-mile 75-minute round trip. Services over the 10-mile Lake Placid section were reintroduced in September 2000 with a return trip taking two hours. Services operate over this section between the end of May and early September The whole line is a project of the Adirondack Railway Preservation Society, a non-profit organization.

Arcade & Attica Railroad

The Arcade & Attica Railroad, incorporated in 1917, is one of a number of U.S. railroads whose primary business remains the movement of freight—in this case primarily agricultural material—but which operates excursion trains in addition. The line's steam-hauled services run on Fridays, Saturdays, and Sundays from May to October from the line's headquarters at Arcade, New York. The round trip of 14 miles runs from Arcade to Curriers, New York. Although there were plans to construct a line as long ago as 1836, it was not until the 1850s that work on the construction of a 3ft 0in (914mm) line commenced although the work was not completed and the line was never opened. A second attempt at completing the line was made in the 1870s, but again this failed. On April 5, 1880, however, the Tonawanda Railroad was incorporated, with backing from the Erie Railroad, to build a 24-mile narrow gauge line. The first train operated from Attica to Curriers Corner on September 11, 1880; the line was extended to Arcade on May 1, 1881, and on September 4, 1882, to Cuba. The various companies formed to build the extensions merged into a single operator—the Tonawanda & Cuba Railroad—but the financial problems that had beset the earlier companies re-emerged, and the line went bankrupt, being sold in April 1894. A new company—the Buffalo, Attica & Arcade Railroad—was formed to take over the line and convert it to standard gauge. The rebuilt line reopened from Attica to Curriers in January 1895. Further extensions followed and, in 1904, the railroad became a subsidiary of the

Buffalo & Susquehanna Railroad, who sold it to the Arcade & Attica Railroad in 1917. Diesel traction was introduced in 1941 and normal passenger services were withdrawn a decade later.

Belfast & Moosehead Lake Railroad

The Belfast & Moosehead Lake Railroad is a 33-mile long branch based in Waldo County, Maine. The line was built in 1867 and is one of the oldest continuously operational railroads in the U.S. Passenger services over the line were fully introduced on December 23, 1870. From 1870 to 1925 the line was operated by the Maine Central Railroad under lease from the B&MLR. However, as the MCR's finances deteriorated, it decided to terminate the lease and, on January 1, 1926, the B&MLR took over operation itself with diesel traction replacing steam in 1946. Scheduled passenger services were withdrawn on March 9, 1960, as the automobile took its toll, although, encouraged by the railroad, freight traffic continued to develop. However, by 1990, the final freight had all but disappeared from the line and, had it not been for a decision in 1988 to reintroduce excursion trains, the line would have closed. The line was acquired in the mid-1990s by Bert G. Clifford and its center of operations moved from Belfast to Unity. Following Clifford's death, the line was acquired by the Railstar Corporation. Excursions operate from Unity, Maine, from early June through to the end of October. Services are either steam—courtesy of a 1912-built Swedish locomotive acquired in 1995—or diesel hauled.

Pages 24–25: "K-36" No. 481 hugs the mountainside as it hauls a service train along the narrow gauge Durango & Silverton Railroad in Colorado. *Derek Huntriss*

Left: The 1913 Swedish-built 4-6-0 pictured in operation on the Belfast & Moosehead Lake Railroad in August 1997. The locomotive was acquired in 1995 and given the name *Spirit of Unity*. *Brian Solomon*

Big South Fork Scenic Railway

Based in Stearns, Kentucky, the Big South Fork Scenic Railway—part of the McCreary County Heritage Foundation (a not-for-profit organization)—operates along a section of the former Kentucky & Tennessee Railway. The railroad is currently in the process of restoring a further section of the line to Worley to use with further plans to extend further, including reopening over the five-arch concrete span over the south fork of the Cumberland River. At present the line is entirely diesel-operated but a steam locomotive—Stearns Coal & Lumber Co. No. 113—is currently under restoration. The line is open primarily from April through to the middle of November with a number of special trains outside this period. There is normally one departure per day, with the round-trip taking about three hours.

Right: Big South Fork Scenic Railway.
Raymond Gehman/Corbis

Blue Ridge Scenic Railway

Based in Blue Ridge, Georgia, the Blue Ridge Scenic Railway operates over a short section of the Marietta & North Georgia Railroad along the Toccoa River. It is a subsidiary of the Georgia Northeastern Railroad, which operates the freight service along the line. Operations commenced in 1998. The round trip, which takes three and a half hours, is 26 miles in length and operates from March to December. All trains are diesel hauled. The history of the line dates back to the late 1880s. The original M&NGR was sold to become the Atlanta, Knoxville & Northern in 1896 before again being sold six years later to become part of the Louisville & Nashville Railroad. Further changes of ownership saw the line ultimately pass to CSX in the 1980s; by this date, however, passenger services over the route had ceased and the freight was the only traffic. In 1990 CSX put the line up for sale and it was acquired by a group of local investors keen to see railroad services preserved in north Georgia.

Boone & Scenic Valley Railroad

Founded in 1983, the B&SVR was established to preserve a section of the Fort Dodge, Des Moines & Southern Railroad. The railroad, based in Boone, Iowa, runs for some 12 miles along the Des Moines River Valley. The first section of the future railroad opened in 1893 before reaching Fort Dodge and Des Moines in 1907, at which time the line was electrified and used as an interurban. However, with the growth in the usage of automobiles, passenger traffic declined and the last interurban trolley cars were operated in August 1955. Thereafter, the line remained open for freight traffic only. This ceased in 1983, and following purchase for $50,000 by the Boone Railroad Historical Society, the first passenger services were launched in November of that year. Among items on display is a Chinese-built steam locomotive dating from 1989, which was the last commercially constructed steam locomotive in the world. In addition to running the scenic railroad using either steam or diesel traction, the B&SVR also operates a limited electrified streetcar service replicating the type of streetcar that existed until the mid-1950s.

Right: The Chinese-built 2-8-2 Mikado-type locomotive—the last commercially built steam locomotive in the world—pictured on the Boone & Scenic Valley Railroad on June 8, 1996. *Brian Solomon*

Branson Scenic Railway

Offering trips through the Ozark Mountains, the Branson Scenic Railway is based in Branson, Missouri, and operates over 20 miles of the erstwhile White River Railway. The line was built originally between 1902 and completion on December 29, 1905; by that date 239 route miles had been constructed with the project costing some $12 million. The development of the railroad encouraged the growth of Branson as a tourist destination for visitors to the Ozark Mountains. The line was part of the Missouri Pacific Railroad between Kansas City, Missouri, and Little Rock, Arkansas, latterly becoming part of the Union Pacific. The line is now controlled by the Missouri & Northern Arkansas Railroad and the Branson Scenic Railroad, founded in 1993, operates it tourist services under a lease to the MNAR. The tourist services, which either operates north from Branson to Galena, Missouri, or south to Barren Fork Trestle, Arkansas, depending on the MNAR freight traffic, are all diesel hauled, with a locomotive positioned at both ends of the train in order to avoid the locomotive having to run-round its stock at its destination. Services operate daily, with the normal exception of Sundays, from March to December.

California Western Railroad

Operating between Fort Bragg, California, and Willits, California, the California Western Railroad—nicknamed the "Skunk Train" after the gas-powered railcars introduced on to the line's passenger services in 1925—operates steam and diesel-hauled passenger services over some 40 miles of line alongside the Noyo River. The standard gauge line was originally opened by the Fort Bragg Railroad in 1885 to carry lumber from Glenela 6.5 miles to a new mill at Fort Bragg; the line remained owned by the lumber company until 1969. In 1904 a passenger service along the line was introduced and, in 1905, the line was renamed the California Western Railroad & Navigation Co. (becoming the California Western Railroad in 1947). The line was completed through to Willits on December 11, 1911. After 1969, the line ultimately became part of the Georgia-Pacific Corporation, which leased the railway operations to Kyle Railways. The line was sold to Kyle Railways in 1987, but by then declining freight traffic and the eventual closure of the Fort Bragg mill meant that the line's future was in doubt as the line's sole revenue was effectively the steam excursion traffic (these services had originally been reintroduced in 1965 using Baldwin-built locomotive No. 45). The line was sold to the Sierra Railroad on December 17, 2003, who continued to operate the excursion services. Services operate between April and December from Fort Bragg and between May and December from Willits and can be steam or diesel operated.

Right: The California Western Railroad is now the home to a number of preserved examples, such as No. M100 illustrated here. *Harry Luff Collection/© Online Transport Archive*

Far Right: Ex-McLoud Railroad diesel No. 55 in use on the California Western Railroad. *Harry Luff Collection/© Online Transport Archive*

Right: No. 45 departs from Fort Bragg with a passenger service. *Harry Luff Collection/© Online Transport Archive*

Far Right: The California Western Railroad acquired the nickname "The Skunk Line"—which its current owners use for marketing the line today—as a result of the introduction of gas-powered railcars in the 1920s. The line still possesses a number of railcars, such as this Budd-built example No. M300 seen at Fort Bragg. *Harry Luff Collection/© Online Transport Archive*

Cass Scenic Railroad

Located in the mountains of West Virginia, the standard gauge Cass Scenic Railroad operates over lines originally constructed for exploiting the area's forests. Based at Cass, West Virginia, the line operates over some 11 miles to just below the summit of Bald Knob (at 4,842ft the third highest peak in the Allegheny Mountains). The town of Cass was founded in 1901 by the West Virginia Pulp & Paper Co., and for a period, the sawmill in the town was the largest in the world. Construction of the network of railroad tracks that served the area started in 1901 and at its peak some 140 route miles was in operation. In 1926 part of the system was sold to the Western Maryland and, 16 years later, the WVP&P sold the remainder of the business to the Mower Lumber Co. By the 1950s, however, the lumber business was in decline, and by the end of the decade, it looked as though the line would be sold for scrap. In 1960, a railfan (Russel Baum), proposed that a section of the line could be preserved as used as a tourist attraction. Initially, the state authorities were reluctant to back the proposal, but following a site visit, greater enthusiasm emerged, and for $125,000, a section of track plus three locomotives and other items of rolling stock were acquired from the scrap merchant. Passenger services were introduced following remedial work in 1963 and the site is now a West Virginia State Park. Services operate from late May through to the end of October with the round trip from Cass to Bald Knob taking some five hours although there are other travel options as well. The line today possesses eight Shay locomotives and two others.

Far Left: Also on display at Fort Bragg was this 2-6-0+0-6-2. *Harry Luff Collection/© Online Transport Archive*

Left: Cass Scenic Railroad No. 5 is one of a number of three-truck Shays based on the line and was built originally by Lima. *Derek Huntriss*

Catskill Mountain Railroad

The Catskill Mountain Railroad links Phoenicia, New York, with Boiceville, New York, and provides a 12-mile round trip along the Esopus Creek in the Catskill Mountains. The standard gauge line was originally built by the Ulster & Delaware Railroad. The route was originally chartered as the Rondout & Oswego in 1866, becoming the New York, Kingston & Syracuse in 1872 and the U&DR in 1875. The line through to Oneonto was completed in 1900. Widely regarded as one of the most scenic lines in the east, the U&DR made much from serving the booming Catskill tourist traffic, although it was also used for coal traffic from northern Pennsylvania into New York City. However, the line's fortunes fell as a result of motor competition in the post-World War I environment and, weakened financially by poor management, the U&DR became part of New York Central in 1932 and, after 1968, part of Penn Central. Selective abandonment led to the complete withdrawal of remaining services by Conrail in 1976. Three years later the line was purchased by the county of Ulster in the hope of attracting a tourist railroad to the line. In 1983, the Catskill Mountain Railroad commenced operations with the line being extended in 2004. At Phoenicia, the historic railroad station, built in 1900, is home to the Empire State Railway Museum. The CMR has long terms plans for further extensions to the line, taking the line's length to 25 miles and connecting Kingston with Phoenicia. Further sections of the line are operated by the Delaware & Ulster Railroad and by the New York State Trolley Museum at Kingston.

Left: Recreating a typical freight train from the age before the line closed in the late 1950s, one of the Cass Scenic Railroad's Shay locomotives is reflected in the river as it descends toward Cass. *Derek Huntriss*

Conway Scenic Railroad

Situated in North Conway, New Hampshire, the Conway Scenic Railroad operates a line that originally dated back to the era immediately after the Civil War. The line from Conway to North Conway opened on June 3, 1872, and two years later was extended to Intervale. The station building at North Conway, built for the Portsmouth, Great Falls & Conway Railroad, was designed by Nathaniel J. Bradlee and opened in 1874. North Conway was a popular tourist destination during the summer months and, in the winter, the line was also used by skiers with snow trains operating from 1932 onward. However, the rising use in automobile ownership meant that passenger traffic declined and services over the route were withdrawn on December 2, 1971. Freight continued for a further decade until this traffic ceased on 30 October 1972. The Conway Scenic Railroad took over North Conway station in 1974 and has subsequently restored it to 19th century splendor. The CSR operates two excursions: North Conway to Conway (11-mile 55-minute round trip) or to Bartlett (21-mile 90-minute round trip)—the "Valley Train"; or from North Conway to Crawford Notch (a five-hour 50-mile round trip) or Fabyan (a five and a half-hour 60-mile round trip)—the "Notch Train." Diesel traction is the norm for services to Bartlett or Crawford Notch, although the line's one steam locomotive—No. 7470—is now back in service after an overhaul and is used on services between Conway and North Conway. Services operate between April and December.

Left: The Conway Scenic Railroad operates in New Hampshire. *Brian Solomon.*

Cumbres & Toltec Scenic Railroad

Based at Chama, New Mexico, the C&TSR provides a tourist service between there and Antonito, Colorado. The line, constructed to the 3ft 0in gauge, extends for some 64 miles and was formerly part of the Denver & Rio Grande Railroad. The line originally opened on October 4/5, 1880, as part of the Rio Grande's San Juan extension but, unlike much of the rest of the Rio Grande's network, was not later converted to standard (4ft 8.5in) gauge. The line was closed in 1969 but, following pressure from preservationists, the states of New Mexico and Colorado jointly bought the 64-mile stretch, along with nine steam locomotives and rolling stock, for $547,120 in 1970 with services being restored by the C&TSR the following year. The railroad is owned by the Cumbres & Toltec Scenic Railroad Commission, an agency authorized by an act of Congress in 1974, with the support of the Friends of the Cumbres & Toltec Scenic Railroad, a non-profit making organization, providing volunteers for conservation and interpretation. The railway's locomotive depot is located at Chama with its carriage sheds at Antonito. Amongst the line's scenic delights is the Toltec Gorge, where the track follow the cliffs some 600ft above the river. Steam-hauled passenger services, using authentic Rio Grande locomotives, run from late May to mid-October, seven days a week.

Right: A double-headed train, with "K-27" class 2-8-2 No. 463 leading, on the Cumbres & Toltec Railroad passes Dalton, Colorado, with a service train. No. 463 is one of only two surviving members of the Baldwin-built "K-27" class to survive and the only one still based on the ex-Denver & Rio Grande. The locomotive is currently out of service. *Brian Solomon*

Right: The powerful shape of one of the Cumbres & Toltec's Mikado 2-8-2s is shown to good effect in this view. *Brian Solomon*

Far Right: A second view of the double-headed service train. No. 463 is one of only two surviving members of the Baldwin-built "K-27" class to survive and the only one still based on the ex-Denver & Rio Grande. The locomotive is currently out of service. *Brian Solomon*

Above: The smoke from the locomotive hangs in the valley as a seven-closed coach and one open coach train trundles along the narrow gauge Cumbres & Toltec Railroad. *Brian Solomon*

Right: The Cumbres & Toltec is home to five members of the "K-36" class of 2-8-2 built by Baldwin for the Denver & Rio Grande in 1925. Apart from No. 484 illustrated here, the line also possesses Nos. 483, 487–489. Of the ten locomotives built, only one number no longer exists: No. 485 scrapped in the mid-1950s. *Brian Solomon*

Left: Class "K-36" No. 484 of the Cumbres & Toltec Railroad pictured at the head of a tourist service near Cresco. *Brian Solomon*

Right: Two of the Cumbres & Toltec's Mikado locomotives—"K-27' No. 463 on the left and "K-37" No. 497 on the right—await their next duties. *Brian Solomon*

Left: "K-36" No. 488 creates dramatic smoke effects as it hauls a passenger service over the Cumbres & Toltec. *Brian Solomon*

Right: The drama of a steam railroad: the headlight at the front of one of the Cumbres & Toltec Railroad's Mikado 2-8-2s illuminates the gloom. *Brian Solomon*

Left: "K-28" No. 463 leads a double-headed excursion on the Cumbres & Toltec. *Derek Huntriss*

Pages 54–55: The lines of the classic "K-36" class silhouetted against the clear blue sky on the Cumbres & Toltec. *Brian Solomon*

Above: A double-headed service, with "K-36" No. 489 leading, on the Cumbres & Toltec. *Jim Livesey*

Right: "K-36" No. 484 at the head of a passenger train on the Cumbres & Toltec. *Brian Solomon*

Left: "K-36" No. 487—arguably the Cumbres & Toltec Scenic Railroad's flagship locomotive—stands at Chama in September 1980. *Harry Luff Collection/© Online Transport Archive*

Right: No. 484 is pictured again, standing adjacent to the water tower at Los Penos. *Harry Luff Collection/© Online Transport Archive*

Left: Two of the Cumbres & Toltec Scenic Railroad's Class "K-36" 2-8-2s, Nos. 484 and 487, double-head a passenger service. *Harry Luff Collection/© Online Transport Archive*

Above: Two of the Cumbres & Toltec Scenic Railroad's Mikado 2-8-2s, Nos. 489 and 497, head a demonstration freight train during a special photographic charter on the line. *Derek Huntriss*

Delaware & Ulster Railroad

Based at Arkville, New York, the Delaware & Ulster Railroad has the potential to operate over some 20 miles of the former Ulster & Delaware Railroad, from Highmount, New York, where it connects with the Catskill Mountain Railroad, and Hubbell Corners, New York. The history of the U&DR is narrated in the section on the CMR (see page 39). Currently, however, it only operates between Arkville and Roxbury as the section to Highmount is out of use as a result of a weak bridge and the section from Roxbury to Hubbell Corners is not of operational standard. The line's most impressive stock is the five-car Budd streamline train, the "Rip van Winkle Flyer," which is used for specials and charters. The majority of ordinary service trains are, however, powered by an Alco-built diesel locomotive. The line is owned, operated and maintained by the Catskill Revitalization Corporation, a non-profit body created for charitable and education purposes. the CRC also controls the 45-mile long linear park—the Catskill Scenic Trail—along the route of the U&DR.

Durango & Silverton Narrow Gauge Railroad

Running between Durango and Silverton, both in Colorado, the Durango & Silverton Narrow Gauge Railroad is one of a number of sections of the erstwhile Denver & Rio Grande Railroad's narrow gauge network to now operate preserved or tourist services. Faced by the challenge of the Rocky Mountains of Colorado ex-Confederate General William Jackson Palmer adopted the 3ft 0in (914mm) gauge for construction of his line south from Denver. Work started at Denver in 1871 heading southward, and by 1872 had reached Pueblo, where Palmer established the Central Colorado Improvement Co., a company which was later to provide the bulk of the line's traffic until the mid-1950s. In 1873 financial troubles led to delays and, by the time that Palmer was able to restart, the most obvious route to the south—the Raton Pass—had already been occupied by another railroad. Palmer then decided to head west, reaching Alamosa via the Sangre de Cristo Range and Veta Pass, in 1878, but again the line's path was blocked by another company's line. In 1879 the courts ruled in favor of the Rio Grande but the railway collapsed financially and the line came under the influence of Jay Gould, who also controlled the Union Pacific. Under Gould's guidance a settlement was reached which allowed the Rio Grande to expand further. However, as the line expanded, Gould's influence declined and Palmer regained control. The section of line now operated by the D&SNG was opened in 1881–82 and has been continuously operated by steam since that date. Unlike much of the ex-Rio Grande network, it was not converted to the standard gauge in the 1890s. The line was acquired by the D&SNGR from the Denver & Rio Grande Western in March 1981. The section between Durango and Chama—see the Cumbres & Toltec Scenic Railroad—has been abandoned. In the summer services operate for the full distance but in the winter months trains only operate between Durango and Cascade Wye.

Left: Denver & Rio Grande No. 473 shunts stock after the completion of a day's working. *P.T. Nunn*

Left: Headed by "K-28" No. 473, a Durango & Silverton service crosses over the Annimos River bridge.
Harry Luff Collection/© Online Transport Archive

Right: The "K-28" class of 1923 was built for the D&RGR by Alco. A total of ten locomotives was constructed of which three now remain. No. 478 is pictured at the head of a train at Durango. *Harry Luff Collection/© Online Transport Archive*

Far Right: Sister locomotive No. 473 is also seen at Durango. Of the ten locomotives, seven were requisitioned by the U.S. Army in 1942 and used on the White Pass & Yukon line. They were scrapped in 1946. *Harry Luff Collection/© Online Transport Archive*

Page 72: The second of the "K-36" class departs with a service to Silverton. *Derek Huntriss*

Page 73: The "480" series "K-36" class of ten locomotives was built by the Baldwin Locomotive Works in 1925 and were the last narrow gauge locomotives constructed in the United States. Designed for freight traffic, the class was used extensively over the narrow gauge network. The first of the class is pictured on the turntable at Durango on October 7, 1993. *Derek Huntriss*

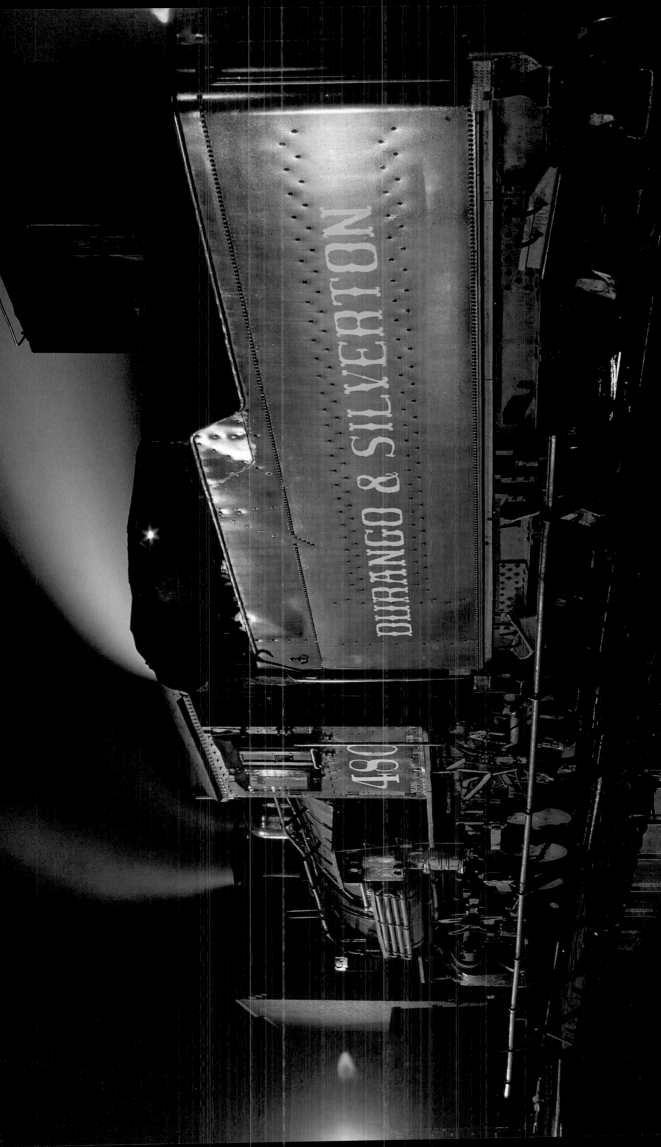

Below: Examples of the two "K" class locomotives stand next to each other. On the left is "K-28" No. 476 and, on the right, "K-36" No. 481. The "K-36" series was more powerful—with a tractive effort of 36,200lb—and heavier—at 286,600lb—than the earlier "K-28" class. *Jim Winkley*

Right: Baldwin No. 15 was built in 1914 and was the third 2-8-2 acquired by the East Broad Top Railroad that year. It is pictured here at the head of a passenger train during August 1987. *Harry Luff Collection/© Online Transport Archive*

East Broad Top Railroad

One of the more curious of the U.S.'s scenic railroads, the East Broad Top Railroad was initially restored in part by the scrapdealer, Nick Kovalchick, who acquired the rights to dismantle the whole route on closure in 1956. Today it is still owned by his scrap company albeit now designated a National Historic Landmark and is on the National Register of Historic Places. Based at Rockhill Furnace, Pennsylvania, the EBTRR is a 3ft 0in (914mm) line that was originally constructed between 1872 and 1874 to convey coal from the Broad Top Mountain plateau to the Pennsylvania Railroad at Mount Union. At its peak, the line possessed 60 miles of track, with a main line stretching for almost 33 miles. With declining demand for coal, the line closed in 1956 and was then sold to the Kovalchick Salvage Corporation; however, it was not immediately dismantled, and in 1960, the boroughs of Rockhill and Orbisonia celebrated their bicentenaries. To mark the event, Kovalchick was asked to display a commemorative train. However, he decided to restore four miles of track and two locomotives, allowing operation over a few months. Such was the success that the service, now extended over five miles, was restored again in 1961 and it has been running each summer since then. The line's services are predominantly operated by steam, but the line also possesses a considerable variety of other 3ft 0in gauge locomotives and rolling stock. Services operate at weekend from the start of June to the end of November. Alongside the line's station at Rockhill Furnace is the Rockhill Trolley Museum, which operates trolleys on the EBT's Shade Gap branch.

Left: Built by Baldwin in 1912, No. 14 was the second Mikado 2-8-2 to be delivered to the East Broad Top Railroad and was more powerful than the earlier No. 12. The locomotive was out of service between 2001 and 2005 for repair but is now operational again. *Harry Luff Collection/© Online Transport Archive*

Above: Again viewed in August 1987, Mikado No. 15 re-entered service over the line in 2005 following a four-year overhaul.
Harry Luff Collection/© Online Transport Archive

Right: Passengers enjoy the experience of a double-headed excursion on the East Broad Top Railroad. *Brian Solomon*

Far Right: All the atmosphere of the traditional railroad roundhouse recreated at the East Broad Top Railroad. *Brian Solomon*

Right: Built by Baldwin in 1912, No. 14 was the second Mikado 2-8-2 to be delivered to the East Broad Top Railroad and was more powerful than the earlier No. 12. The locomotive was out of service between 2001 and 2005 for repair but is now operational again. *Brian Solomon*

Left: Built by Baldwin in 1911, No. 12 was the first and smallest "Mikado" 2-8-2 to enter service with the East Broad Top Railroad. Named *Millie* in 1960, this popular locomotive is currently out of service. *Brian Solomon*

Right: East Broad Top No. 15, the third 3ft 0in (914mm) gauge 2-8-2 to be built by the Baldwin, makes an impressive sight as it departs with a service train in the autumn of 2000. *Derek Huntriss*

Left: An atmospheric shot of steam and smoke on the East Broad Top Railroad as the locomotive runs light engine. *Brian Solomon*

Right: East Broad Top No. 17 was the second largest Mikado, 2-8-2, to be delivered to the line. Built in 1918, the locomotive was the only heavy Mikado to be restored for use on the line, although the locomotive is currently out of use and stored. *Brian Solomon*

Right: East Broad Top
Railroad: the line was
initially sold in 1956 to
the Kovalchick Salvage
Corporation for
dismantling but, in
1960, the first stirrings
of restoration occurred
when the boroughs of
Orbisonia and Rockhill
sought a limited display
to mark their
centenaries. *Brian
Solomon*

Far Right: Today the
line remains in the
ownership of the
Kovalchick Salvage
Corporation and is
perhaps unique among
U.S. tourist railroads in
that it is a complete
original railroad rather
than a collection
gathered together from
disparate sources.
Brian Solomon

Fillmore & Western Railway

Based at Fillmore, California, and nicknamed "Home of the Hollywood Movie Trains" (as the locomotives and stock were largely acquired from three of the U.S.'s leading film companies and the line's operators have had some 40 years of experience in dealing with the provision of locomotives and rolling stock to the movie industry), the Fillmore & Western operates excursions over the Union Pacific line through the Santa Clara Valley. The F&WR has been based at Fillmore since the mid-1990s when the operator moved its collection of historic locomotives and rolling stock to the city as part of the authority's efforts to regenerate the city's business center after the 1994 earthquake. The line was originally part of the Southern Pacific's main line but the importance of the route declined following the opening of the Montalvo cut-off through the Santa Susana Mountains in 1924. All the excursion services are diesel-hauled.

Fremont & Elkhorn Valley Railroad

Running for some 17 miles between Fremont and Hooper in Dodge County, Nebraska, the Fremont & Elkhorn Valley Railroad operates over track originally opened by the Fremont, Elkhorn & Missouri Valley Railroad in 1869. The original line continued through to Norfolk and then to Fort Robinson, in the north of the state. A westward extension saw the line reach western Wyoming, near Yellowstone Park. The original company merged with the Chicago & Northwestern in 1903 and it was the C&NW that closed the route in the 1980s. Following closure, the section from Fremont to Hooper was acquired by the Nebraska Railroad Museum, a not-for-profit organization, whose volunteers now operate the service. The section of line to Wyoming is now being converted into a long-distance trail—the "Cowboy Line." The standard gauge line is operated by diesel locomotives and services operate between late May and the end of October with normally one return working each Saturday and Sunday.

Georgetown Loop Railroad

The narrow-gauge Georgetown Loop Railroad, part of the Colorado Central Railroad (later Colorado & Southern), was one of Colorado's first tourist attractions when it opened on March 10, 1884. The line remained open for passenger and freight traffic until 1938 when it closed; the line was subsequently dismantled. Almost 40 years after closure, work started on reopening a four-mile section in 1973 with material donated by the Union Pacific Railroad; this was achieved in 1984. Work included the reconstruction of the high bridge, which stands some 95ft above the valley bottom. The four-mile long line climbs some 640ft in its journey.

Left: A double-headed passenger train crosses the 95ft high trestle bridge as it makes its way along the Georgetown Loop Railroad. The line originally closed before World War II and was dismantled; restoration work, including the construction of a new trestle bridge, led to the line being reopened for tourist services in 1984. *Derek Huntriss*

Far Left: Locomotive No. 12, a 2-6-2 originally built for the Kahului Railroad, hauls a passenger train on the Georgetown Loop Railroad on October 3, 1993. *Derek Huntriss*

Grand Canyon Railway

Running between Williams, Arizona, and the South Rim of the Grand Canyon, this standard gauge line has been providing tourist passenger services since 1989. The line originally opened on September 17, 1901, when the Achison, Topeka & Santa Fe Railway's branch from Williams formally opened. Passenger services were operated until July 1968 when the Santa Fe withdrew them, although the line remained open until 1974 for freight traffic. Earlier attempts at the line's reopening failed and it was not until 1988, when the line was acquired by Max and Thelma Biegert, that restored services became a reality. Passenger services over the 64-mile line were reinstated, appropriately, on September 17, 1989, and the line now carries almost a quarter of a million passengers annually. Apart from the line itself, there is also a museum on the Grand Canyon Railway based at the station in Williams. The Biegerts remained owners until late 2006 when the enterprise was sold to Xanterra Parks & Resorts, a company based in Denver, Colorado.

Above Right: Unseasonable May weather as the Grand Canyon Railroad's No. 10 leaves Williams, Arizona, at the start of its trip to the Canyon. *John Vaughan*

Right: A pair of vintage Alco diesel locomotives, headed by No. 6773, arrives at Williams, Arizona, in May 1996. *John Vaughan*

Far Right: A few hours' lay-over at the Grand Canyon rail site for the railroad's Alcos before the train returns to Williams. *John Vaughan*

Right One of the Grand Canyon Railroad's operational 2-8-0s, No. 29, is pictured in the workshops at Williams, Arizona, on April 12, 1990. *Gavin Morrison*

Far Right: Pictured alongside ex-Santa Fe diesel No. 2769 on April 12, 1990, is Grand Canyon Railroad No. 18; this locomotive is currently out of service. *Gavin Morrison*

Great Smoky Mountains Railroad

Running from two stations—Dillsboro and Bryson City, North Carolina—the Great Smoky Mountains Railroad operates over the western part of the former Murphy branch of the Southern Railway and skirts the southern border of the Great Smoky Mountains National Park. The operator is a subsidiary of American Heritage Railways, which also operates the Durango & Silverton. The line operates a tourist service all through the year using either its one steam locomotive—2-8-0 No. 1702—or diesel traction. In addition to operating a tourist passenger service, the line also carries a limited amount of freight. The line was the scene of one of the more dramatic scenes featuring railroads in film: the accident during which Harrison Ford escapes in the 1993 film *The Fugitive* was shot at Dillsboro and the set can still be seen alongside the line.

Work started on the construction of the 116-mile long Murphy branch of the Western North Carolina Railroad from Asheville in 1881. The line required many engineering works, including the 836ft Cowee Tunnel to the west of Dillsboro, and was built by convicts supervized by armed warders. During construction, a number were killed in accidents, including 19 drowned in the Tuckasegee River while constructing the tunnel. The line opened for services in 1884. The line saw its heaviest use during the 1940s with the construction of the Fontana Dam, but the same decade also witnessed the withdrawal of passenger services—on July 16, 1948—when Southern Railway, the line's then owners, ceased to operate them as a result of road competition. With freight traffic also in decline, in 1985 Norfolk Southern closed the line from Dillsboro through to the terminus at Murphy. The line and track were acquired by the state of North Carolina and from 1988 onward tourist services were launched over the Dillsboro to Nantahala section. The railroad operates a variety of excursions using both steam and diesel traction.

Right: Excursions on the Great Smoky Mountain Railroad can be either steam or, as illustrated here, diesel-hauled. *Will & Deni McIntyre/Corbis*

Hawaiian Railway

Based on the Hawaiian island of Oahu, the Hawaiian Railway currently operates over some 6.5 miles of track. Operated by the Hawaiian Railway Society, a non-profit organization founded in 1970 to preserve the island's railway history, services over the line are diesel hauled although the society does own a number of steam locomotives—none of these have as yet been restored to an operational condition. Services operate throughout the year on Sundays, with charters available on Mondays to Saturdays. The normal round trip takes about 90 minutes with all services starting from Ewa.

Left: A Hawaiian Railway trains nears Kalaeloa Boulevard. The five "coaches" being hauled were all constructed on old railway flats donated by the military. *John Vaughan*

Heber Valley Historic Railroad

Operating between Heber City, Utah, and Vivian Park, in Provo Canyon, the Heber Valley Historic Railroad runs over part of the Denver & Rio Grande branch linking Heber City with Provo, which opened originally in 1899. The standard-gauge line was to survive until complete closure in 1967 after which it was acquired for tourist services—and steam excursions along the route commenced in 1970. The original promoter of these services failed financially in the late 1980s and the line was secured via a non-profit organization—the Heber Valley Historic Railroad Authority—established in the early 1990s. The section between Provo and Bridal Veil Falls was abandoned prior to the creation of the HVHRA and is now a footpath. The section between Vivian Park and Bridal Veil Falls, some two miles, was abandoned in the late 1980s as a result of its condition but was not actually lifted until 1996. Steam-hauled services through the Provo Valley operate throughout the year, with the return trip taking some three hours. In addition to the line's normal program of excursions, a number of special events are also held throughout the year.

Lahaina-Kaanapali & Pacific Railroad

Based on the Hawaiian island of Maui, the Lahaina-Kaanapali & Pacific Railroad operates over a six-mile stretch of former sugar cane railroad from Lahaina to Puukolii via Kaanapali. The round trip from Puukolii to Lahaina, including a 45-minute break at Lahaina, takes almost three hours. Passenger services have been operated over the line since 1970 and, in that time, more than five million passengers have traveled over the route. The line's origins date back more than a century to the growth of the island's sugar industry, when the line was used to haul sugar cane to the processing factories and workers to the fields. Among the line's attractions is the 325ft-long wooden trestle bridge that offers stunning views of the neighboring islands and of the West Maui islands.

Far Left: On the lovely island of Maui is the Lahaina-Kaanapali & Pacific Railroad. Steam services run between Lahaina Town and the resort of Kaanapali. *John Vaughan*

Left: Trains on the Lahaina-Kaanapali & Pacific are marketed as the "Sugar Cane" train. Blasting out of Lahaina Town is this impressive 3ft 0in gauge 2-4-2T with its train of three coaches. *John Vaughan*

Manitou & Pike's Peak Railway

Located in Colorado, the Manitou & Pike's Peak Railway is the highest in the U.S. Constructed using the Abt rack system, the central cog is designed to aid traction as the train ascends the average 16 percent gradient toward the 14,100ft summit of Pike's Peak. The line, promoted by Zalmon Simmons as a tourist line from the start, was opened in two stages: to Halfway House Hotel in 1889 and to the summit in 1890. Initially the line was operated by steam, with locomotives supplied by Baldwin. These were fitted with inclined boilers to ensure that they were kept level while ascending and descending the mountain. In 1938 the railway acquired a petrol-driven railcar—believed to be the first supplied to any rack railway in the world—and from 1940 onward, acquired diesel-powered locomotives. These were designed to supplant the steam locomotives, which were increasingly expensive to maintain, although a number of steam locomotives were retained until the 1960s. In 1964 the railroad's fleet was further enhanced by the purchase of two new railcars, produced in Switzerland, and two further were acquired later in the decade. In 1974, as traffic continued to increase, further rolling stock, in the guise of two two-car articulated units, was again acquired from Switzerland. The M&PPR runs four to six return workings per day between mid-May and September, with fewer services during the rest of the year.

Right: When first opened, the Manitou & Pike's Peak was steam hauled; one of the Baldwin-built locomotives, superseded by more modern traction from the 1930s onward, stands preserved at Manitou station. *Harry Luff Collection/© Online Transport Archive*

Far Right: Pike's Peak Railroad No. 16 stands at the summit—some 14,000ft above sea level. *Harry Luff Collection/© Online Transport Archive*

Mid-Continent Railway

Based at North Freedom, Wisconsin, the Mid-Continent Railway operates over a seven-mile, 50-minute round trip through the scenic Baraboo Hills. Services operate from May to October. Currently, all the line's steam locomotives are out of action and so all services are at present diesel hauled. Services have been operated over the line since 1963 by a non-profit organization, the Mid-Continent Railway Historical Society. Originally founded in 1959, the 4.2-mile long line was acquired from the Chicago & North Western in 1963. The collection encompasses current 13 steam locomotives, 38 diesel locomotives and more than 100 items of rolling stock.

Right: Chicago & North Western Class R-1 4-6-0 No. 1385, originally built in 1907, pictured on the Mid-Continent Railway in 1994. *Brian Solomon*

Right: Mid-Continent's ex-Chicago & North Western 4-6-0 recorded again, on February 18, 1996. *Brian Solomon*

Far Right: Saginaw Timber 2-8-2 No. 2 photographed on the Mid-Continent Railway in 1995. This is one of the museum's extensive collection of steam locomotives. *Brian Solomon*

Left: The Mid-Continent Railway is based at North Freedom, Wisconsin, and operates over track previously owned by the Chicago & North Western. No. 1385 is pictured in service on the line on October 14, 1995. *Brian Solomon*

Pages 106–107: Two more views of the Mid-Continent Railway. *Brian Solomon*

Midland Railway (Kansas)

Based at the 1906-built Atchison, Topeka & Santa Fe depot in Baldwin City, Kansas, the standard gauge MR was established in the early 1980s with the intention of preserving a stretch of abandoned railroad track. It purchased the 11-mile long line from Baldwin to Ottawa, Kansas, in 1987 and began operating passenger services later that year, with excursion trains operating over the entire route from 2004. The line over which the railroad operates was originally opened in 1867 and services, which are diesel hauled, normally operate from June through to the end of October.

Mount Hood Railroad

Situated in Oregon, some 60 miles east of Portland, the Mount Hood Railroad operates tourist services through the Hood Valley between Hood River, where the line meets the Union Pacific Railroad, and Park Dale—a distance of some 21 miles. The standard gauge line was originally opened from Hood River to Dee in 1906 and extended from there to Park Dale three years later. The line was acquired by Union Pacific in 1968 but, with the decline of freight traffic, proposed closure. However, the line was acquired in 1987 by its present owners, who operate diesel-hauled services along the route. The railroad also operates a limited freight service and, for 2007, a 1910-built steam locomotive will provide motive power for the tourist trains.

Right: Mount Hood No. 88, originally Southern Pacific No. 3885, is one of two EMD "GP9" locomotives based on the line. *Richard Hamilton Smith/Corbis*

Mount Rainier Scenic Railroad

Normally operating from Elbe, Washington, to Mineral, Washington, the Mount Rainier Scenic Railroad operates over a seven-mile stretch of line. However, due to track damage at the Nasqually River bridge, the operation for 2007 is scheduled to operate south from Mineral to Divide. This route is six miles long and the round-trip takes between 60 and 90 minutes. Some services, however, will operate between Mineral, Divide, and Morton; this is a 30-mile round trip and the return journey takes some four hours. The main feature of the line beyond Divide is the wooden trestle bridge located south of Divide. The non-profit organization that operates the tourist services over this standard-gauge line is dedicated to preserving the region's railroading history and possesses a number of geared steam locomotives specifically designed to operate over the steeply graded lines used in the local logging industry. Normally, all tourist trains are scheduled to be steam-hauled although the line does also possess some diesel locomotives. The line operates over a route built by the Tacoma Eastern Railroad between 1902 and 1910. On December 31, 1918, the line became a subsidiary of the Chicago, Milwaukee & St Paul Railroad, who continued to operate the line until closure in 1980; tourist services operated by the Mount Scenic Railroad, part of the Western Forest Industries Museum, commenced the same year.

Mount Washington Cog Railway

One of only two cog railroads in the U.S., the Mount Washington, in New Hampshire, predates the other—the Manitou & Pike's Peak—by some 20 years. Promoted by Sylvester Marsh, who climbed the mountain in 1857, the project to build the railroad was widely considered to be impossible. The first section of the line opened in 1868 with the summit (6,288ft) being reached the following year. The railway, with an average gradient of 25 percent (and a maximum of 37.41 percent), is the second steepest rack railroad in the world. Initially, the steam locomotives had vertical boilers but these were later replaced by locomotives with inclined boilers. During the line's history there have been two fatal accidents: in 1929, during a test run of a restored vertical-boilered locomotive, one crew member was killed as the locomotive careered down the line following an axle break and, in 1967, eight passengers were killed when the train derailed one mile from the summit. Today, the Mount Washington Railway operates a fleet of eight steam locomotives, dating from 1874 through to 1983.

Right: A Mount Washington Cog Railway train pictured near the summit of the line in July 1964. *Harry Luff Collection/© Online Transport Archive*

Far Right: Mount Washington No. 6 pictured at the summit in July 1971; the view shows to good effect the arrangement of the inclined boiler—essential if a steam locomotive is to operate safely over gradients encountered on lines such as the Mount Washington. *Harry Luff Collection/© Online Transport Archive*

Right: The Napa Valley
Wine Train is normally
hauled by one the line's
FPA-4 locomotives built
at the Montreal
Locomotive Works and
originally delivered in
Canadian National
Railway. *Gavin Morrison*

Napa Valley Wine Train

Operated by the Napa Valley Railroad since 1989, this standard gauge service is a privately run excursion train that works alongside Route 29 in California from Napa through the towns of Yountville, Rutherford, and Oakville to St. Helena. The round trip is 37 miles and the journey takes three hours, the original Napa Valley Railroad was founded in the early 1860s to carry tourists to Calistoga from Vallejo. The line was sold to the California Pacific Railroad on June 9, 1869, and renamed later the same year. The track was leased to the Southern Pacific Railroad on April 1, 1885, and extended to meet the SPR at Suisin. Ownership passed formally to the SPR in 1898 and the line was partially electrified four years later with electric services reaching Calistoga in 1912. Passenger services were withdrawn in 1929 with the line then utilized by freight traffic until closure in 1987. It was at this point that local entrepreneurs, in the face of some local opposition, set out to launch the wine train. Today, diesel-hauled services operate.

Right: No. 72 is pictured on a service; the train's consist normally includes nine coaches, which include dining, lounge, and observation cars. *Gavin Morrison*

Inset Right: The Napa Valley Wine Train logo as carried by locomotive No. 72. *Gavin Morrison*

Far Right: O. Winston Link was undoubtedly one of the greatest of U.S. railroad photographers; with his distinctive use of black & white films and flash lights, his style is instantly recognizable. This view of Baldwin-built 4-6-0 No. 40 on the Nevada Northern Railroad recreates the style of railroad photography that Link pioneered. *Gordon Osmundson/Corbis*

Nevada Northern Railway

Copper was initially discovered in the area in 1902, and the railway was originally constructed to serve the copper mines and smelter of the Nevada Consolidated Copper Co. in White Pine County, Nevada, the standard gauge NNR is based in Ely, Nevada. The railroad first reached Ely in 1905, and by 1910, the line was complete and passenger and freight services introduced. Passenger services were to survive until 1941 but copper traffic continued until 1983 when the copper company, now known as the Kennecott Copper Corporation, closed its mining operations. Diesel traction replaced steam from 1948 onward. Following closure, the White Pine Historical Railroad Foundation was established; this received substantial donations—including 32 miles of track—from Kennecott and, three years later, the newly restored steam locomotive No. 40—nicknamed the "Ghost Train of Old Ely"—re-entered service. This locomotive was originally built by Baldwin in 1910 and is one of three steam locomotives based on the line. The line also possesses a number of diesel locomotives. Passenger services operate from Ely either north to Adverse or west to Keystone, depending on the date of travel and time of departure. Generally, steam is used on the line to Keystone with diesel traction being used to Adverse (the Hiline Route).

New Hope & Ivyland Railroad

Running between New Hope and Lahaska, Bucks County, Pennsylvania, the 17.5-mile long New Hope & Ivyland Railroad operates most Fridays and weekends throughout the year and daily during the months of June through October. The line's history has been somewhat chequered as a tourist operation, although it first operated a tourist service as long ago as August 6, 1966. The original NH&IR had been formed to acquire the line from the Reading Railroad for a sum of $200,000, but suffered financial problems in the early 1970s and, in 1974, the Bucks County Industrial Development Corporation took over ownership, although both tourist passenger and freight services continued to operate. A further change of ownership in 1990 saw the BCIDC sell the line to a new company, the Bucks County Railroad Preservation & Restoration Corporation, a for-profit enterprise that undertook a $2 million restoration of the route; in 1991, steam-hauled passenger services were reintroduced. Steam motive power is provided by 2-8-0 No. 40 although the line also possesses a number of diesel locomotives; the diesels are usually used in the winter months when No 40 undergoes maintenance.

New Hope Valley Railway

Based in Bonsal, North Carolina, the NHVR runs for a distance of six miles between there and New Hill, North Carolina. The line posses six diesel locomotives and one steam locomotive along with a range of rolling stock. The line was originally constructed in 1905–06 by the New Hope Valley Railway in order to exploit the timber reserves of the valley and provide a link for the communities along the line with the Seabord Air Line Railroad at Bonsal. The line was extended southward from Bonsal to Duncan between 1911 and 1913, where it formed a connection with the Norfolk Southern Railroad. In 1917 the NSR took out a lease on the line, and eight years later, a branch was opened from Durham to serve a new tobacco factory in the city. The original alignment of the line was abandoned in the 1970s when it was rebuilt on a new route by the U.S. Corps of Engineers in connection with the construction of the B. Everet Jordan Dam. The line was briefly owned by the Southern Railway before the Bonsal-New Hill section was sold for preservation on January 15, 1982, following the cessation of SR revenue earning services the previous year. Services resumed in 1984. North of New Hill the trackbed of the line constructed by the Army Corps of Engineers has been converted into the American Tobacco Trail. The majority of the line's locomotive stock are diesel-powered, although the line does possess one steam locomotive—an 0-4-0T, No. 19, built by the Vulcan Iron Works in 1941.

Left: Steam power requires the use of cylinders and valve gear to transmit the pressure in the boiler to tractive effort on the railroad. This close-up view shows part of the valve gear of a steam locomotive in use on the Nevada Northern Railroad. *Gordon Osmundson/Corbis*

Niles Canyon Railway

Operating between Sunol and Fremont through Niles Canyon in California, the Niles Canyon Railway utilizes a former Southern Pacific Railroad line closed originally in 1984 between Niles and Sunol stations. Work commenced on restoring the track by the Pacific Locomotive Association—a not-for-profit organization dedicated to preserve the atmosphere of Pacific coast railroading in the years between 1910 and 1950—reaching Niles in 1987 and the first tourist service ran on May 21, 1988. The association has, at the time of writing, a collection of some 10 steam and 13 diesel locomotives, with both types of traction being used on the line's excursion services. Services over the line operate on Sundays only, weekly during the summer months and less frequently in the period of January to March and October to November; there are no services in December. A single journey takes about 30 minutes with the round trip taking 90 minutes in all. The line was originally built by the Western Pacific Railroad with the first section, from San Jose to Alameda Creek—some 20 miles—being opened on October 2, 1866. However, construction was then delayed until 1869 when the line was completed through to Sacramento by the Central Pacific Railroad, which had earlier acquired the WPR. The CPR was later taken over by the Southern Pacific, which possessed a main line to the north—through Benicia and Martinez—and therefore put little investment into the alternative ex-CPR route.

Left: California Western Railroad railcar No. M200 pauses on the Niles Canyon Railway. The line operates over a former Southern Pacific line in the West Bay area of California. *John Vaughan*

Far Left: The New Hope & Ivyland Railroad's steam-hauled services are handled by 2-8-0 No. 40 between April and December. During the months of January to March the locomotive undergoes maintenance during which period services are diesel hauled. The locomotive served previously on the Cliffside and Lancaster & Chester railroads. *Derek Huntriss*

North Shore Scenic Railroad

Operating between Duluth, Minnesota, and Two Harbors, Minnesota, the standard gauge North Shore Scenic Railroad is operated by the Lake Superior Railroad Museum. The railroad operates a number of excursions, of which the longest is the 52-mile round trip between Duluth and Two Harbors along the northern shore of Lake Superior. The round trip, which takes six hours, includes a two-hour break at the eastern terminus. The line's origins date back to the late 19th century and the development of the local iron industry.

Opened in 1886, the Lakefront Line, as it was known, provided a link between isolated Duluth & Iron Range Railway with the rest of the network courtesy of a one-mile link between the Lakefront Line and the St. Paul & Duluth Railway. Passenger services, which included a shortlived suburban service from Duluth to Lester Park (which operated from 1887 to 1892), were dieselized in 1953 with steam being replaced by a Budd railcar. The final passenger services were withdrawn in 1961. Freight continued, however, until the 1980s when the Duluth, Missabe & Iron Range Railroad, as successor to the D&IRR, sought permission to close the route. However, the line was preserved with the backing of the state and, on June 8, 1989, the line was officially renamed the North Shore Scenic Railroad. The Lake Superior Railroad Museum is the line's third operator since then, having operated the route since 1996.

Right: Ex-Duluth & Northern Minnesota Railway No 14 recorded on the North Shore Scenic Railroad on July 6, 1996. *Brian Solomon*

Old Colony & Newport Scenic Railroad

Located in Newport, Rhode Island, the Old Colony & Newport Scenic Railroad operates a standard gauge service through the Newport RI Naval Base and along the Narragansett Bay. Services offer a 10-mile round trip from the line's main station at 19 America's Cup Avenue in Newport and pass a pass a number of major US warships—including the aircraft carriers U.S.S. *Saratoga* and U.S.S. *Forrestal*—that are displayed within the naval base. The line over which the service operates was authorized on April 9, 1861, with through services over the completed line commencing on February 1, 1864. At its peak the line carried some 24 passenger trains a day but, after World War I with the rise of the private automobile, passenger levels declined and scheduled services ceased in 1938. Freight traffic continued thereafter but again these were to decline, particularly by the 1960s. The line's then owner, the New Haven Railroad, went bankrupt in 1968 and its assets passed to Penn Central and the new owner eventually filed for abandonment. The state of Rhode Island eventually acquired the southernmost 19 miles of the line. The line is currently operated by the National Railroad Foundation & Museum, a non-profit organization, and services operate throughout the year. All services are diesel hauled although passengers travel in coaches dating to before World War I.

Osceola & St. Croix Valley Railway

Based at Osceola, Wisconsin, the Osceola & St. Croix Valley Railway, part of the Minnesota Transportation Museum, has been in operation since September 5, 1992. The normal service operates from April to October from April through to October from Osceola through the St Croix Valley to Marine, a distance of some ten miles. This part of the trip takes 90 minutes. On its return to Osceola, the train then heads east to Dresser, a distance of a further five miles. In addition to these sections, the railroad also has operational rights over the 9.5 miles onward from Marine to the junction at Withrow, Minnesota, and the 15 miles from Dresser to Amery. It has, over the years, operated specials over these lines. The MTM established its operations at Osceola following the demise of its earlier St. Paul & Stillwater Railroad, which had failed as a result of the lack of community support, and set up the non-profit O&SCVR in partnership with the Osceola Historical Society. Freight traffic from the quarry at Dresser still operates over the line to Withrow, operated by Wisconsin Central (a subsidiary of Canadian National since 2001), although the section from Dresser to Amery was closed by Wisconsin in 1998. Passenger services are hauled by one of the three MTM diesel locomotives based on the line.

Right: Northern Pacific No. 328 is part of the Minnesota Transportation Museum collection, of which the Osceola & St. Croix Scenic Railway is part. The locomotive was one of a batch of ten 4-6-0s delivered from Alco in February 1907; only two locomotives of the type survived the Great Depression, with the remainder being cut up between 1929 and 1933. In 1946, the only other survivor—No. 321—was also scrapped, leaving No. 328 as the sole representative of the class before withdrawal in 1950. Slated for scrapping, the locomotive was, however, to survive as a static exhibit at Stillwater, Minnesota, before being restored to operational condition between 1976 and 1981. *Brian Solomon*

Far Right: Northern Pacific Class S-10 4-6-0 No. 328 pictured at Dresser. The locomotive is currently out of action and is being overhauled with a view to a return to steam. The locomotive is based at the MTM's Jackson Street roundhouse while this work is completed. *Brian Solomon*

Potomac Eagle Scenic Railroad

Centered at Romney, West Virginia, the Potomac Eagle Scenic Railroad—owned by Dave Corbitt and Dan Snyder—operates over a section of the closed Baltimore & Ohio line from Green Spring to Petersburg, West Virginia. The tourist service operates over the South Branch Valley Railroad, established by the state in 1978 to replace B&O, and tourist services commenced in 1991. The highlight of the trip is a the journey alongside the South Branch of the Potomac River, through "The trough," an area which is famous for sightings of bald eagles. The South Branch Valley Railroad—based in Moorefield and owned by the state and which operates the remaining freight traffic over the line—extends for just over 52 miles from Petersburg to Green Spring, where it connects into the main line from Cumberland, Maryland, to Martinsburg, West Virginia. It was originally opened by the South Branch Railroad on September 1, 1884. The line passed to the Moorefield & Virginia Railroad in 1911 and to the Baltimore & Ohio in 1913. Passenger services over the line ceased in the late 1920s. B&O closed the line in the mid-1970s and it was taken over by the state on October 11, 1978. Since then the State Rail Authority has undertaken considerable investment in the line, particularly in restoring it after serious flood damage in 1985. All the line's tourist services are diesel hauled with the normal excursion operating from Wappocomo station, north of Romney, some 8.5 miles to Sycamore Bridge. The 17-mile round trip takes some three-and-a-half hours.

Rio Grande Scenic Railroad

Located at the center of the San Luis Valley, Alamosa, Colorado, was at the center of a network of narrow gauge lines constructed by the Denver & Rio Grande Railroad. The lines serving Alamosa were eventually converted to standard gauge and passed, via various mergers, to the Southern Pacific and Union Pacific in 1996. The 154-mile section now owned by the San Luis & Rio Grande Railroad, a subsidiary of Permian Basin Railways established in 2003, was sold by RailAmerica to PBR in 2005. The Rio Grande Scenic Railroad, a joint venture between the SL&RGR, the Denver & Rio Grande Historical Foundation, and the Chambers of Commerce of Alamosa and La Veta, runs two passenger services. The "San Luis Express" operates between Alamosa and La Veta; this service was inaugurated in 2006 over a section of line that had last seen passenger services in 1953. The second train, the "Toltec Gorge Limited," runs from Alamosa to Antonito, where a connection with the C&TSR is made. Both trains operate daily, with one return working each. All trains are diesel-hauled.

lines, originally built to the 3ft 0in gauge, opened to Alamosa on June 22, 1878. From here the line was extended through to Antonito—see the section on the Cumbres & Toltec Scenic Railroad—in 1880, and thereafter, Alamosa saw further narrow gauge lines constructed. Unlike the future C&TSR, the lines serving Alamosa were eventually converted to

Right: Durango & Silverton "K-28" No. 478 makes smoke as it hauls a passenger service through the dramatic scenery of Colorado. *Jim Sugar/Corbis*

Roaring Camp & Big Trees Narrow Gauge Railroad

One of two railroads based in Felton, California, owned by Roaring Camp Railroads, the RC&BTNGR is a 2.5-mile long 3ft 0in (914mm) gauge line that runs from the line's depot at Felton to the summit of Bear Mountain through second-growth Redwood forest. The line operates throughout the year, with services daily from March to the end of October. The line has been operational as a heritage route since 1963, when the late F. Norman Clark (1835–1985) established it; the line is currently owned and managed by Clark's widow, Georgina. The railroad possesses a number of both steam and diesel locomotives, with services normally in the hands of one of the line's Shay locomotives.

Right: One of the Roaring Camp & Big Trees NGR's two-truck Shays, No. 1 *Dixiana*, is pictured in the line's shed. This locomotive was built by the Lima Locomotive Corporation in 1912 and acquired from Virginia in 1962. *Harry Luff Collection/© Online Transport Archive*

Far Right: RCBT No. 2 *Tuolumne* is a two-truck Heisler and was built in 1899 by the Stearns Manufacturing Co. It was acquired in 1963 but is used relatively infrequently due to the high cost of maintenance. *Harry Luff Collection/© Online Transport Archive*

Far Left: Also recorded in the line's shed is No. 3 *Kahuku*. This is a Baldwin-built 0-4-2T locomotive dating to 1890 and acquired in 1966 from the Kahuku Plantation in Hawaii. *Harry Luff Collection/© Online Transport Archive*

Left: Heisler No. 2 is recorded at the head of a passenger service as it passes under one of the two wooden trestle bridges, one of the line's scenic highpoints. *Harry Luff Collection/© Online Transport Archive*

Left: The line originally crossed the trestle bridges as part of a loop, but the wooden structures were seriously damaged by fire in 1976, four years before this 1980 view, and were replaced by a switchback to enable the line to reopen for its full length. *Harry Luff Collection/© Online Transport Archive*

Below: No. 2 recorded at the head of a passenger train. Apart from a number of steam locomotives, the Roaring Camp & Big Trees NGR also operates a number of diesel locomotives. *Harry Luff Collection/© Online Transport Archive*

Royal Gorge Route Railroad

Offering a two-hour—three-hour for the dinner trains—excursion over the most famous portion of the Denver & Rio Grande Western Railroad from Canon City, Colorado, the Royal Gorge Route Railroad provide a 24-mile round trip through some of the most spectacular scenery in the U.S. Fought over by both the Denver & Rio Grande and the Santa Fe railroads (literally at times), the Royal Gorge, to the west of Canon City, was the only route through the high plateau through which a railway could be constructed to reach the Leadville area where prospectors were eagerly seeking silver and lead; even so, the gorge offered serious difficulties for the railroad builders of the late 19th century. Between 1878 and 1880 both the D&RGR and the SF sought to obtain the sole route through the gorge; eventually, the D&RGR proved successful but only after the involvement of the federal courts. On March 27, 1880, the two railroads signed an agreement—nicknamed the "Treaty of Boston"—that paved the way for the D&RGR to complete the line to Leadville. this opened on July 20, 1880. The line was originally constructed to the narrow gauge but, like much of the D&RGR, was later converted to standard gauge. Normal passenger services over the line were withdrawn in July 1967. All services are diesel-hauled and operate from March to May (weekends only) and May to October (daily). In addition, there are also a number of special services, such as the dinner train service that operates in the evening.

Right: All services over the Royal Gorge Route railroad are diesel-hauled but offer superb vistas to passengers during their 24-mile round trip. *Richard T. Nowitz/Corbis*

Far Right: Baldwin-built No. 12 of the North Pacific Coast Railroad is one of a number of narrow gauge rolling stock on display at the California State Railroad Museum in Sacramento. The Museum's collection is used to provide the standard gauge locomotives and rolling stock used on the Sacramento Southern Railroad. *Wolfgang Kaehler/Corbis*

Sacramento Southern Railroad

Based at Sacramento, California, the Sacramento Southern Railroad is a standard gauge tourist line that operates over part of the former Southern Pacific Railroad line from Sacramento to Freeport. The line, which has seen a heritage service since 1982, is operated by the California State Railroad Museum from its base at Sacramento. Steam-hauled services operate every weekend from April to the end of September and offer a six-mile round trip taking 40 minutes from the Central Pacific Freight Depot in Old Sacramento along the east bank of the Sacramento River. Apart from the regular weekend services, the line also operates a number of specials during the year. The original line extended beyond Freeport to Walnut Grove, a distance of just over 23 miles. The line was originally constructed between 1906 and 1912 with services commencing over the partially completed line in 1909 with full services operating between Sacramento and Walnut Grove on March 12, 1912. In February 1912, just before the line's complete opening, it was sold by SP to the Central Pacific Railway, becoming that company's Walnut Grove Branch. During the 1920s, as competition from both road traffic and rail increased, so the level of service declined although, in order to encourage further traffic, the branch was extended to Isleton in 1929 and to an asparagus cannery on the Mokelumne River two years later. The Great Depression, however, saw normal passenger services withdrawn in 1932 although freight traffic was to continue thereafter. However, severe flooding in 1971 destroyed much of the railroad around Isleton, making much of the route impassable. Traffic gradually declined. Much of the route was formally abandoned in 1977 and, in 1978, the SP applied to close all but the final three miles into Sacramento with a final train operating on October 10 to remove any remaining freight cars. The California State Railroad Museum stepped in and, following successful excursions operated in 1982 and 1983, acquired the line for operation of tourist services.

Sandy River & Rangeley Lakes Railroad

Located in Franklin County, Maine, the 2ft 0in (610mm) gauge SR&RLR was a network of some 112 miles that was created following a number of mergers by narrow gauge railways in the area between 1908 and 1911. The promoter of the lines, George Mansfield, had been inspired by the narrow gauge lines in Wales. The use of the narrow gauge allowed for cheaper construction. The lines included the Sandy River Railroad (the first part of the network to be constructed, opening originally in 1879), the Kingfield & Dead River Railroad, and the Eustis Railroad. Following the rise of road transport during the 1920s, the economics of the railroad declined and the lines were closed, with the final section being abandoned in 1935. Following closure, the track was dismantled, and there the story would have remained except for the creation, in 1970, of a group within the Phillips Historical Society interested in the railroad. The intention was to recreate part of the original line at Phillips, and the contemporary SR&RLR is a non-profit division of the PHS. While much of the original equipment and infrastructure was dismantled at closure, the new SR&RLR, which reopened over a short section of track in the mid-1980s, has relocated a number of original buildings to its site and services are hauled by an original locomotive, No. 4, built by the Portland Engine Co. in 1886.

Santa Cruz, Big Trees & Pacific Railway

The second tourist line controlled by the Roaring Camp Railroads, the Santa Cruz, Big Trees & Pacific Railway is also based in Felton, California. A standard gauge line, the SCBT&PR operates through the Henry Cowell Redwoods State Park and down the San Lorenzo River Gorge before terminating at Santa Cruz

Beach Boardwalk. The tourist service has been operational since 1985. Normal services operate from the end of May to the end of September, with specials running in November and December. All services are diesel-operated and operate from Olympia to Santa Cruz Wye, where the line meets the Union Pacific line, and thence to Santa Cruz Beach Boardwalk over the metals of the UP line from Watsonville to Davenport. The SCBT&PR is one of the few tourist lines in the U.S. with significant amounts of track in the middle of city streets. The line was originally opened by the narrow-gauge Santa Cruz & Felton Railroad in 1875 to shift lumber from the mountains to the Bay. It was later taken over by the South Pacific Coast before being acquired by the Southern Pacific. It was the gauge prior to World War I. Part of the route beyond Olympia was closed in 1940 as a result of flooding, leaving the Olympia-Santa Cruz section to continue until 1981 when further flooding led to its closure. It was acquired by Norman Clark, who died in 1985, and was reopened fully some years after his death

Sierra Railroad (Railtown 1897 State Historic Park)

Railtown 1897 State Historic Park is based at Jamestown, California, and is home to one of the last authentic operating railroad roundhouses in the United States. In addition to the roundhouse, the site also offers visitors the opportunity to travel behind a steam locomotive on excursions operated most weekends between April and October (with selected weekends in November and December). The exhibits held at Jamestown represent the California State Railroad Museum's collection and include locomotives, rolling stock as well as other material relating to the history of railroading in the state. The round-trip is some six

miles in length, from Jamestown to Rock Spur, taking some 40 minutes in rural. All services are scheduled to be steam hauled. The line over which the service operates was incorporated as the Sierra Railway of California on January 1, 1897, and construction of the first 41 miles from Jamestown to Oakdale commenced on March 24, 1897. The section into Jamestown was completed on November 10, 1897. Services between Jamestown and Sonora started on February 26, 1899. The bulk of the line's revenue came from the local lumber industry but the Sierra's final expansion—taking total route mileage to some 140 miles—was as the result of projects to construct dams on the Tuolumne and Stanislaus rivers in the 1920s, and the building of the O'Shaughnessy Dam in the following decade. However, decline was in the air and, by the end of the decade, all passenger services had been withdrawn and the first sections of track abandoned. With its proximity to Hollywood, the line developed a new form of traffic—the movie business—and therefore retained historic equipment, stored at Jamestown, for this type of work. Although the line was dieselized in 1955, the traditional steam roundhouse at Jamestown was retained and this was sold for preservation to the State of California in 1982 along with the historic locomotives and rolling stock it contained. The track over which the special trains operate is now owned by the Sierra Railroad and the excursion services operate under an agreement between the railroad and the State of California.

Above: Smoke to order for the movie makers! Known as the "Movie Railway," the Sierra Railway is regularly hired out to film makers. *John Vaughan*

Right: Hard-working Shay No. 2, built in 1922 and a gift to the collection in November 1967 from the Georgia-Pacific Corporation, runs between Chinese Camp and Jamestown in June 1996. *John Vaughan*

Far Left: Flying the flag! Sierra Railroad's Baldwin 2-8-0 No. 28 runs round its train at Chinese Camp in July 1993. *John Vaughan*

Left: Many preserved railroads used small internal-combustion service vehicles to attend lineside fires. This example is based on the Sierra Railroad. *John Vaughan*

Strasburg Railroad

Stretching for 4.5 miles, the Strasburg Railroad is the oldest surviving short-line tourist railway in the U.S.. Based in Strasburg in Lancaster County, Pennsylvania, the railroad runs from there to Leamans Place. The line's history stretches back to incorporation on June 9, 1832, although its not certain when operation actually started. The first recorded timetable is dated December 1851 and passenger services did not commence until February 22, 1861, when President Lincoln visited Leaman. Passenger services continued until the first decade of the 20th century when competition from the new Conestoga Traction Co.'s trolley route from Lancaster to Strasburg hit the passenger business hard. Freight remained, however, but even this was to decline forcing the 1957. A local rail enthusiast, Henry K. Long, established a not-for-profit organization that purchased the line for $18,000 on November 1, 1958. Limited freight services were restored on November 11, 1958, and on January 4, 1959, tourist passenger services were launched. The railroad has a number of operational steam locomotives and the round trip takes some 45 minutes. In the summer months the railroad is one of the few locations in North America where two steam locomotives are in operation simultaneously.

Right: One of a number of engines that once operated on the Strasburg Railroad, but which are no longer based there, the 1223 is seen at on the Strasburg in 1983. The locomotive, built in 1905, operated over the Strasburg Railroad from 1965 until 1990. *Jim Livesey*

Far Right: The Strasburg Railroad recorded in 1996. *Brian Solomon*

Pages 142-143: The Strasburg Railroad in 1997. *Brian Solomon*

Upper Hudson River Railroad

The standard-gauge Upper Hudson River Railroad operates alongside the Hudson River in New York State with its headquarters at North Creek. Services operate from North Creek and run to Riparius over the track of the erstwhile Adirondack Railroad. Construction of the original line commenced in 1865 and North Creek was reached in 1871. The AR became part of the Delaware & Hudson Railroad in 1889 with North Creek remaining the terminus until World War II when the line was extended a further 30 miles in order to serve a mine at Tahawus. The mine kept the line operational until 1989 when it closed. Then the D&H abandoned the railroad and it lay derelict for a decade. In order to develop tourism, Warren County purchased the track with the intention of operating a tourist service over it. The following year the Upper Hudson River Railroad was contracted to operate a service from North Creek over 8.5 miles to Riverside station, Riparius, with the ultimate intention of extending services over some 40 miles of line. Services over the line, which are diesel hauled, operate from May to October and take two hours for the return journey

Valley Railroad (Connecticut)

Operational since July 29, 1971, this Connecticut-based tourist line operates over some 23 miles of former Penn Central track between May and the end of October from Essex, Connecticut. Outside the main season the line operates a number of specials services. Many of the services operate in conjunction with a riverboat, the round trip involving both modes of transport taking some 2.5 hours. Services are operated by the Valley Railroad company. The line over which the trains operate was constructed by the Valley Railroad with work commencing in 1870. The complete 45-mile route from Hartford was completed the following year and the first train operated on July 29, 1871. Following the receivership of the original company in 1876, the line passed to Hartford & Connecticut Valley Railroad on July 1, 1880, and in 1892, the line passed to the New Haven Railroad. It was to be owned by the NHR until the new owner itself collapsed financially in 1961 although freight traffic continued to operate until complete closure came to the Valley Railroad in 1968, by which stage the assets were owned by the Penn Central. Volunteers endeavored to prevent the line being dismantled and on August 15, 1969 Penn Central passed the line over the state of Connecticut. A formal lease, covering the 23 miles from Essex up the Deep River, was granted to the Valley Railroad Co. on June 1, 1970, and the following year steam-hauled services were reintroduced.

Page 144-145: Built by Baldwin Locomotive Works in 1906, 4-8-0 No. 475 was originally constructed for the Norfolk & Western Railroad. It has been operational on the Strasburg Railroad since 1993. *Derek Huntriss*

Right: Valley Railroad (Connecticut) 2-8-2 Mikado No. 40. *Brian Solomon*

Right: The Valley Railway (Connecticut) operates over some 23 miles of former Penn Central track out of Essex, Connecticut. *Brian Solomon*

Far Right: One of the Valley Railroad's currently operational steam locomotives is ex-Aberdeen & Rockfish Railroad No 40, a 2-8-2 Mikado originally constructed by Alco. The locomotive was built originally in 1920 and acquired by the A&RR in 1935. It was sold to the Valley Railroad in 1977. *Brian Solomon*

Verde Canyon Railroad

Located near Clarkdale, Arizona, the Verde Canyon Railroad was originally opened in 1912 as the Verde Valley Railway. The line, which cost $1.3 million to build, was constructed in a year by 250 men using 200 mules and a considerable quantity of explosives. Built to service the copper mines at Jerome, Arizona, the 38-mile long line was operated by the Santa Fe Railway until closure in 1989. Taken over by Dave Durbano, 20 miles of the line from Clarkdale to Perkinsville reopened to provide tourist passenger services in November 1990. The trip, taken by some 60,000 passengers annually, takes four hours and runs alongside the Verde River for its entire journey with two national forests alongside and is the only means of gaining access to the dramatic Verde Canyon. The trains are diesel-hauled and there is normally one return working per day although occasionally two trains, one in the morning and one in the afternoon, are operated.

Virginia & Truckee Railroad

Located with its base in Virginia City, Nevada, the Virginia & Truckee currently operates for some 2.5 miles from Virginia City to Gold Hill, although there are plans to extend the line a further 17 miles to Carson City. The extension will traverse spectacular scenery including the Carson River Canyon. The line's origins date back to the discovery of silver and the need to move the ore from the mines to the processing mills in Carson City. Work started on the line in 1870 and was completed the following year; the construction, which employed some 1,500 laborers mostly Chinese, cost some $1.5 million and included the construction of five tunnels. With the decline in the silver industry came the loss of the railway with the Virginia City section closing in 1938 and the entire railroad 12 years later. Despite being abandoned, the growth of tourism encouraged the development of a project to reopen the route, and in 1974, work started on the line's restoration, with passenger services commencing three years later. Today, steam-operated tourist services operate between May and the end of October. It is estimated that complete restoration of the line through to Carson City, scheduled for completion by the end of 2010, will cost some $40 million.

Left: No. 8 is a 2-6-2 locomotive built for the Feather River Railroad on display at the Virginia & Truckee Railroad in Nevada. *James L. Amos/Corbis*

Right: Pictured leaving Virginia City, Nevada, is Baldwin-built 2-8-0 No. 29 with a train bound for Gold Hill. *John Vaughan*

Page 152: Viewed from the train's open carriage, the Virginia & Truckee's Baldwin No. 29 descends towards Gold Hill with a train from Virginia. Gold Hill is the current terminus of the line but there are ambitious plans that will see the line once again connect Virginia to Carson City. *John Vaughan*

Page 153: A Virginia & Truckee Railroad train pictured at Gold Hill Depot headed by No. 29, a 2-8-0 built originally by the Baldwin Locomotive Works for the Longview, Portland & Northern Railroad. *© Jan Butchofsky-Houser/Corbis*

West Chester Railroad

The standard gauge West Chester Railroad operates over some seven miles of former Pennsylvania Railroad track between Market Street, Pennsylvania, and Glen Mills, Pennsylvania. The line is controlled by a non-profit organization, the West Chester Railroad Heritage Association. The line over which the WCR operates was originally the West Chester & Philadelphia Railroad, which opened on November 11, 1858. The line became part of the PR in 1881, becoming known as the PR's Media branch. The line was electrified by the PR in 1927 and continued to carry passenger services until these were withdrawn early in 1986. The track lay derelict for almost a decade until plans for its restoration started to develop. All services over the line are diesel hauled. Regular services operate on Sundays between early June and the end of September with the round trip taking some 90 minutes. In addition, the line also operates a range of special services.

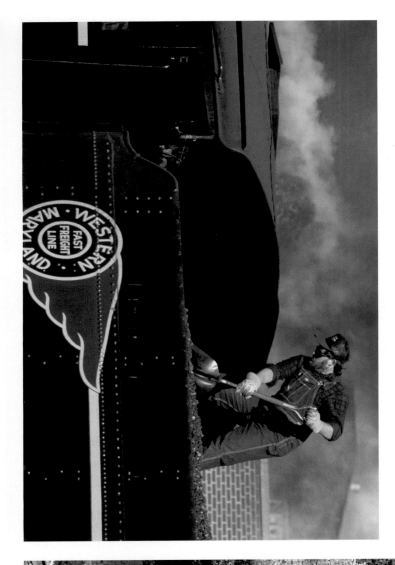

Below: A fireman shovels coal in the tender of the Western Maryland's Scenic Railroad's sole steam locomotive. *Paul A. Souders/Corbis*

Western Maryland Scenic Railroad

Linking Cumberland, Maryland, with Frostburg, Maryland, this tourist railway runs over the lines of the former Western Maryland Railway and was reopened in 1989. Cumberland station, opened originally in 1913, is the line's base and, from here, the line runs through the deep gorge, known as "the Narrows," created by the Wills Creek as it passes between Wills Mountain and Haystack Mountain. This gap in the Allegheny front was the U.S.'s first gateway to the west, being used by the Baltimore & Ohio and the Cumberland & Pennsylvania railroads in addition to the WMR. The line continues through, via Mount Savage, Helmstetter's Curve in Cash Valley, Brush tunnel and Woodcock Hollow to terminate at the old C&PR station at Frostburg, which opened originally in 1891. In addition to running ordinary services, the WMSR also operates murder mystery excursions. Normal motive power for the line is a 1916-built 2-8-0 steam locomotive originally constructed by Baldwins for the Lake Superior & Ishpeming Railroad, which was acquired in 1991 and rebuilt before entry into service the following year.

Left: A 2-8-0 Consolidation type pictured at Helm Stedders Curve on the Western Maryland Scenic Railroad in 1997. *Brian Solomon.*

Left: Originally built by the Baldwin Locomotive Works in 1916, No. 734 was designed primarily for freight traffic and was constructed for the Lake Superior & Ispeming Railroad. After withdrawal the locomotive was acquired by the Illinois Railroad Museum from where the Western Maryland Scenic Railroad acquired it in 1991. Following restoration, the 2-8-0 entered service the following year. *Derek Huntriss*

West Side & Cherry Valley Railroad

As discussed in the introduction, railroad preservation in the U.S. and the operation of heritage or tourist services is perhaps more commercial than in other countries. Over the years a number of lines or services have been promoted only for them to fail. One such example was the West Side & Cherry Valley Railroad based near Tuolumne in California. As with a number of lines featured in this book, the WS&CVR's origins were closely interlinked with the development of the lumber industry in the late 19th and early 20th centuries. The 3ft 0in gauge line originally opened in 1900 and, by 1949, had extended to a total of some 72 miles of track. However, again as elsewhere the decline in the lumber industry resulted in the decline and closure of the railroad. By the time that the West Side Lumber Company closed its railroad on June 7, 1961, the line represented the last narrow-gauge logging railroad still operational in the American west. Following closure, there were efforts—most notably by Glen Bell, the founder of Taco Bell—to resurrect the line as a tourist line but all ultimately failed. Locomotives from the line can be found in use at a number of other narrow gauge lines in the U.S. However, despite the dereliction and dispersal of the line's locomotives and rolling stock, there remains an active restoration society exists aiming to reopen part of the route.

Right: West Side & Scenic Valley Railroad No. 15 was originally built by Lima in 1913. This locomotive can now be seen operating on the Yosemite Mountain & Sugar Pine Railroad. *Harry Luff Collection/© Online Transport Archive*

Opposite page, Above: Another Lima-built three-truck Shay, West Side & Scenic Valley Railroad No. 7 was built originally in 1911. This is one of a number of locomotives from the line that can now be seen in operation elsewhere—in the case of No. 7, the locomotive is currently in operation on the Roaring Camp & Big Trees Railroad. *Harry Luff Collection/© Online Transport Archive*

Opposite page, Below: West Side & Scenic Valley No. 15 is pictured again; the line originally possessed 15 steam locomotives. Of these, no fewer than eight have found alternate homes following the line's closure. *Harry Luff Collection/© Online Transport Archive*

White Pass & Yukon Railway

The first section of this 3ft 0in (914mm) gauge railway was opened on July 21, 1898, to run from the port of Skagway to Whitehorse, Yukon Territory in Canada, to serve the Klondike goldrush. The line was eventually extended to a total of 571 miles to reach Dawson City. Declining traffic resulted in the line's closure in 1982, but the first 20 miles from Skagway to White Pass were reopened for tourist traffic in 1988 and, ultimately, a total of 111 miles to Whitehorse have been reopened for tourist services. Currently, daily services, from the start of May to the end of September operate over the route from Skagway to White Pass, with the 40-mile round trip taking some three hours. During the journey, the train ascends to the Summit at White Pass, some 2,865ft above sea level. Also operated are longer distance services from Skagway to Carcross in Yukon Province; this is a 67.5-mile long single journey for which proof of citizenship is required as the U.S.-Canadian border is crossed. The single journey takes six and a half hours. Other journey options, some involving motorcoaches or hiking, are also offered as is a 52-mile round trip hauled by steam between Skagway and Fraser Meadows; this again requires proof of citizenship and takes four hours to complete. The majority of services are diesel hauled although steam is used on the Skagway-Fraser Meadows service and the line possesses three steam locomotives, of which two are operational, for this service.

Above Right: Based in Alaska, the weather can be a significant factor in the operation of the line, and snow is a considerable threat; this snow-blower is designed to keep the line open during the most adverse weather conditions. *Michael S. Lewis/Corbis*

Right: One of the few preserved railroads to cross an international boundary, the White Pass & Yukon Railway is a narrow-gauge line based at Skagway in Alaska. Baldwin-built No. 73, a 2-8-2, is one of a number of 3ft 0in (914mm) gauge locomotives that operate the line. *Michael S. Lewis/Corbis*

Far Right: Not all the White Pass & Yukon's services are steam hauled, as shown in this view of a double-headed diesel service crossing the wooden trestle bridge at White Pass. *James Marshall/Corbis*

Whitewater Valley Railroad

Situated in Indiana, the WVR has been operational as a heritage railway since the 1970s, when the route over which it operates was closed by Penn Central. The origins of the line date back to the construction of the Whitewater Canal, which opened to Connersville, Indiana, in 1845. Never wholly successful, the Indianapolis & Cincinnati Railroad acquired the rights to build a railroad—the White Water Valley Railroad—alongside the canal in 1863; the line to Connersville opened in early 1867 and was extended to Hagerstown the following year. The line joined the main I&CR at Valley Junction, 17 miles west of Cincinnati. Following a brief period of independence, the WWVR was taken over the Cleveland, Cincinnati, Chicago & St Louis Railroad in 1890. In 1931 the section beyond Connersville was abandoned with passenger services over the remainder of the route being withdrawn two years later. Local freight services over the line were withdrawn by Penn Central—as successor to the NYC in 1968—in 1972. By this date, a not-for-profit organization—the Whitewater Valley Railroad—had been established, which began passenger services over 25 miles of leased track in 1974. However, following flooding, the section between Metamora and Brookville, some four miles, was lifted in 1976 leaving the WVR to operate over the 18 miles from Connersville to Metamora. The WVR acquired the line in 1983, following the cessation of final freight services, and today operates diesel hauled services between Connersville and Metamora with a second service, a two-mile shuttle, operating south from Metamora.

Right: Wilmington & Western 2-6-0 No. 92 recorded during a run from Greenbank to Mount Cuba, Delaware. *H. Bongaardt*

Wilmington & Western Railroad

Based at Marshalltown, Delaware, the Wilmington & Western Railroad operates over some ten miles of standard gauge tracks. The original line was incorporated in 1867 and opened on October 19, 1872, between the port of Wilmington and the mills along the Red Clay Creek to Landenberg, Pennsylvania—a distance of almost 20 miles. However, financial ruin followed and the line acquired new owners in the late 1870s—the Delaware Western Railroad. This, in turn, became part of the Baltimore & Philadelphia Railroad—part of the massive Baltimore & Ohio—in the 1880s, a move which presaged the line's most profitable period as it provided the B&O with a line to compete with the Pennsylvania Railroad for traffic to New York. Passenger services were withdrawn over the route on September 28, 1930, a victim of the Great Depression, and thereafter, with road traffic competition increasing, the all-important freight also started to decline. In the early 1940s, the section from Southwood, Delaware, to Landenberg closed completely with the section between Hockessinn, Delaware, and Southwood following in the late 1950s. From 1966, Historic Red Clay Valley began operating steam-hauled tourist trains over the section from Greenbank to Mount Cuba, but in the mid-1970s, the line's then owners—the Chessie System—sought to close the line completely. However, the HRCV sought to raise funds to purchase the remaining section and, in 1982, bought the remaining ten-mile section. As a result of flood damage caused by storms associated with Hurricane Floyd in 1999 and Tropical Storm Henry four years later, a number of the line's bridges were destroyed, and a gradual program of replacement is in hand. At present, therefore, the line's operations are again restricted to the Greenbank-Mount Cuba section. Excursions are hauled by either steam or diesel traction. The railroad possesses three steam locomotives as well as two diesel-electrics and one diesel railcar.

Yosemite Mountain Sugar Pine Railroad

Constructed in the 1960s by Rudy Stauffer, the Yosemite Mountain Sugar Pine Railroad largely follows the route of the erstwhile Madera Sugar Pine Lumber Company near Fish Camp, California, which operated a narrow gauge line between 1899 and 1931. Constructed to serve the local lumber industry, the line was operated by five wood-fired Shay locomotives that hauled massive log trains to the timber mill. The reconstruction currently houses two Shay locomotives, acquired from the Westside Lumber Company, and these haul most of the line's passenger services; the line also possesses railcars that are used for out of season traffic. The steam locomotives have been converted to oil burning. Services over the four-mile route run daily from the middle of March to the end of October. Today the line is operated by the founder's son Max.

Far Left: Built in January 1909 by the American Locomotive Company, 4-4-0 No. 98 is pictured arriving at Greenbank in October 1996. *Harry Luff Collection/© Online Transport Archive*

Left: Services over the Yosemite Mountain Sugar Pine Railroad were inaugurated using three-truck Shay No. 10, shown here. The locomotive was built in 1928 and was amongst the last narrow-gauge Shay locomotives constructed. It was acquired secondhand from the West Side Lumber Company. *J. Winkley*

Yreka Western Railroad

Operating over some 7.5 miles from Yreka, California, the Rocky Mountain Railroad & Mining Museum of Denver, Colorado, runs a steam special—the "Blue Goose." The train operates once a day on Wednesday through Sunday from June onward. The line operates one steam locomotive—No. 19—but also possesses a number of diesel locomotives.

Construction of the Yreka Railroad commenced in 1888, following the decision of the Central Pacific Railroad to bypass the city, and the line was opened on January 9, 1889. Shortly before U.S. entry into World War I, the railroad changed its name to the Yreka Western as it developed plans—never completed—to extend the line, but the condition of the route deteriorated and, in a virtually moribund condition, it was sold to the Klamath River Holding Co. in 1928. The new owners again proposed to extend the line, but the worsening economic conditions after the Wall Street Crash of 1929 again put paid to the proposed western extension. Between 1935 and 1948 the line was in receivership, but the growth in the local lumber industry restored the line's prosperity. The line was dieselized in 1958 with the remaining two steam locomotives, Baldwin 2-8-2s Nos. 18 and 19, placed on standby: two years later, the company introduced steam-hauled excursions, which continued until the end of the decade. Following a period based on the Oregon Pacific & Eastern Railroad, No. 19 returned to the line in 1988; the following year, the steam excursion trains were reinstated. By the 1990s, the gradual elimination of the lumber industry resulted in the line being threatened with complete closure in 1999. Following local pressure, the line was acquired by a non-profit organization—the Rocky Mountain Railway & Mining Museum—and some 15,000 traveled on the "Blue Goose" in its first season under RMR&MM control. Since the Museum took control, the story has not been a wholly happy one and this resulted in a temporary cessation of the "Blue Goose" service. This was, however, restored for the 2006 season.

Yuma Valley Railway

The standard gauge Yuma Valley Railway is an Arizona-based heritage railway that operates between Yuma and Gadsden along the Colorado River levee. The railway was originally owned by the U.S. Department of the Interior's Bureau of Reclamation and represented part of the department's irrigation and flood control project along the river. Originally known as the Yuma Valley Railroad, the line stretched from Yuma for some 25 miles to the border with Mexico at San Luis. After government ownership, the line passed to the Southern Pacific in 1947. The nine-mile section from Gadsden to San Luis was already out of use by that date and was subsequently abandoned. The line was embargoed by the Bureau of Reclamation in 2005 and the excursion service is currently no longer operating. When services operated, they were diesel hauled and the round trip lasted some two hours with passengers being offered good views of the flora and fauna of the West Wetlands Park, the only National Heritage Area west of the Mississippi. Services operated October to May and in June by appointment only; the line was closed between July and September.

Left: No. 19, a 2-8-2 of the Yreka Western Railroad, recorded in light steam. The line originally dated to 1887 and was used by preservationists in recent years running the "Blue Goose" special out of Yreka. After running into financial difficulties, the line is scheduled to reopen in 2007 *John Vaughan*

Page 168–169: Promontory Summit, Utah, was the point at which the Golden Spike, marking the completion of the first transcontinental line, was driven in. Replicas of the two locomotives concerned are displayed at the site and regular re-enactments of the ceremony are held. *Panoramic Images/Getty Images*

Above: Ex-Chicago, Burlington & Quincy No. 5629 preserved at the Colorado Railroad Museum. *Harry Luff Collection/© Online Transport Archive*

Right: Farmingdale, New Jersey, is this 3ft 0in (914mm) gauge 2-6-2 originally built by the Baldwin Locomotive Works. *Derek Huntriss*

Railroad Museums

Apart from the scenic railroads described in this volume, the U.S. also possesses a large number of museums that feature railroad locomotives and equipment but which do not operate regular tourist services. The following is a list of some, but not all, of these sites.

• Arizona Railway Museum—based at Chandler, Arizona, this collection is dedicated to the history of railroads in Arizona and the southwestern U.S.

• B&O Railroad Museum—situated at Mount Clare, considered to be the birthplace of US railroading, this collection incorporates some 250 locomotives and rolling stock along with some 15,000 artifacts. Following heavy snow in 2003, part of the roof covering the 1884 roundhouse collapsed, destroying certain exhibits beyond repair. The building has been subsequently repaired and there is a program of restoration for those exhibits less seriously damaged.

• California State Railroad Museum—based at Old Sacramento, California, and with operations located at the nearby Sacramento Southern Railroad, this collection houses some 21 locomotives and railroad cars.

• Colorado Railroad Museum—located at Golden, Colorado, near the foot of

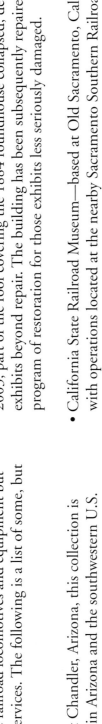

North Table Mountain, this collection includes the largest collection of 3ft 0in (914mm) gauge equipment in North America. It houses some 12 locomotives and over 80 items of rolling stock, both standard and narrow.

• Empire State Railway Museum—housed at the Ulster & Delaware Railroad's historic station at Phoenicia, New York, the museum's collection includes a steam locomotive, No 23, being restored for future use on the Catskill Mountain Railroad.

• Golden Spike National Historic Site—located at Promontory Summit, Utah, this site marks the point at which the two transcontinental lines—the Central Pacific and the Union Pacific—met on May 10, 1869. Replicas of the two locomotives involved are displayed and re-enactments are undertaken during the season.

• Illinois Railway Museum—the United States' largest railroad museum is situated in Union, Illinois, 55 miles northwest of Chicago, the collection houses some 400 locomotives and items of rolling stock. The museum operates railroad services over a five-mile stretch of line between April and October and also operates a on-mile streetcar loop.

Far Left: A replica of Union Pacific No. 119 preserved at Promontory Summit, Utah, at the point at which the golden spike was inserted alongside...
P. J. Howard

Left: ...Central Pacific Jupiter, another replica constructed to mark the centenary of the ceremony.
P. J. Howard

• Indiana Railway Museum—situated at French Lick, Illinois, the collection houses some 65 locomotives and items of rolling stock. Passenger services are operated over the section of ex-Southern Railway track between French Lick and Cuzco—the French Lick Scenic Railway—from April to November. The return journey through part of the Hoosier National Park takes just over two hours. All services are diesel-hauled.

• Indiana Transportation Museum—based at Noblesville, Indiana, the museum

Left: Rio Grande Southern No. 20 is a 3ft 0in gauge locomotive and is preserved as part of the Colorado Railway Museum Collection. *Brian Solomon*

Below: Another static exhibit at Steamtown is ex-Canadian Pacific 4-4-4 No. 2929, which was built originally in 1938. *Harry Luff Collection/© Online Transport Archive*

Left: The Steamtown collection includes more than 30 steam locomotives, although many are not operational. This impressive display gives some idea of the scale of the museum's collection. *Harry Luff Collection/© Online Transport Archive*

Above: The Baldwin Locomotive Works at Philadelphia was one of the United States' main builders of steam locomotives, and many preserved examples can be seen throughout the country. This is a typical builder's plate proudly proclaiming the locomotive's origins. *Brian Solomon*

operates over the metals of the erstwhile Indianapolis & Peru Railroad with services operating between May and December. Services can be either steam or diesel hauled.

- Kentucky Railway Museum—comprising some ten locomotives and over 100 items of rolling stock, this collection is housed in New Haven, Kentucky. Passenger services are operated over an 11-mile section through the Rolling Fork River Valley from March to December.

- Lake Superior Railroad Museum—situated at Duluth, Minnesota, the collection includes some 20 locomotives and more than 40 items of rolling stock.

- Minnesota Transportation Museum—occupying the 1907-built Jackson Street roundhouse in St. Paul, Minnesota, this collection houses a number of ex-Northern Pacific steam locomotives, plus other locomotives—both steam and diesel—and other items of railway interest. The museum has close connections with the Osceola & St Croix Valley Railway.

- Museum of Transportation—sited in St. Louis, Missouri, the Museum of Transportation has a large collection of locomotives and rolling stock both from the state and elsewhere in the U.S. It also houses other forms of transport, such as automobiles.

- Museum of the American Railroad—this large collection is based in Dallas, Texas, and includes some 12 locomotives as well as many other items of rolling stock.

- National Railroad Museum—sited at Ashwaubenon, Wisconsin, the National Railroad Museum is one of the oldest railroad museums in the U.S. Its large collection includes a Class A4 Pacific from Great Britain—a sister locomotive to No. 4468 *Mallard* which holds the world record for the fastest steam locomotive in the world.

- Nevada State Railroad Museum—situated in Carson City,

Above: Northern Pacific 4-6-0 No. 328 recorded at the Minnesota Transportation Museum on August 17, 1996. *Brian Solomon*

Right: Part of the extensive collection held at Steamtown, Scranton, Pennsylvania, is ex-Canadian Pacific No. 2317 seen at the head of a special. *Derek Huntriss*

Left: Union Pacific No. 6946 is one of a large number of ex-Union Pacific diesel locomotives displayed at the Western Pacific Railroad Museum in California. *Gavin Morrison*

Below : A general view of the Western Pacific Railroad Museum at Portola, California, taken on July 2, 1994 shows part of the museum's extensive collection of historic locomotives. *Gavin Morrison*

Nevada, the museum also operates the Nevada Southern Railroad at Boulder City, Nevada. The museum's collection include some 65 locomotives and items of rolling stock, many constructed for use by the Virginia & Truckee Railroad.

- New Jersey Museum of Transportation—based at Farmingdale, New Jersey, this collection houses a number of steam and diesel locomotives.

- Northern Pacific Railway Museum—this small museum based at Toppenish, Washington, includes an ex-Northern Pacific locomotive, No. 1364 (currently undergoing restoration) and a collection of ex-Northern Pacific memorabilia.

- Northwest Railway Museum—located in Snoqualmie, Washington, this museum possesses some 19 steam and diesel locomotives as well as other items of rolling stock. The museum operates passenger services from April to October over a five-mile stretch of line in the Upper Snoqualmie Valley.

- Ohio Railway Museum—based in Worthington, Ohio, this museum is one of the oldest railroading museums in the U.S., dating back to 1948. The museum operates a one-mile demonstration line for its electric streetcars and includes some 30 steam, diesel and electric vehicles in its collection.

- Oklahoma Railway Museum—situated in Oklahoma City, Oklahoma, this museum houses both steam and diesel locomotives. It operates diesel-hauled passenger services.

Right: A trio of the line's locomotives—"K-36" No. 481 and two "K-28s" Nos. 478 and 476—are recorded on shed at the Durango & Silverton Railroad. *Aurora/Getty Images*

- **Railway Museum of Greater Cincinnati**—Sited at Covington, Kentucky, the collection includes some 80 items of motive power and rolling stock.

- **Railroad Museum of Pennsylvania**—located slightly to the east of Strasburg, Pennsylvania, this collection houses more than 100 locomotive and railroad cars.

- **Steamtown**—incorporating two original roundhouses, this museum is situated on the site of the former Scranton yards of the Delaware, Lackawanna & Western Railroad in Scranton, Pennsylvania.

- **Virginia Museum of Transportation**—sited at Roanoke, Virginia, the museum incorporates a number of locomotives and other items of railroading interest.

- **Western Pacific Railroad Museum**—located at Portola, California, the collection encompasses some 35 diesel locomotives from the Western Pacific, Union Pacific and Southern Pacific along with one steam locomotive built for the Western Pacific.

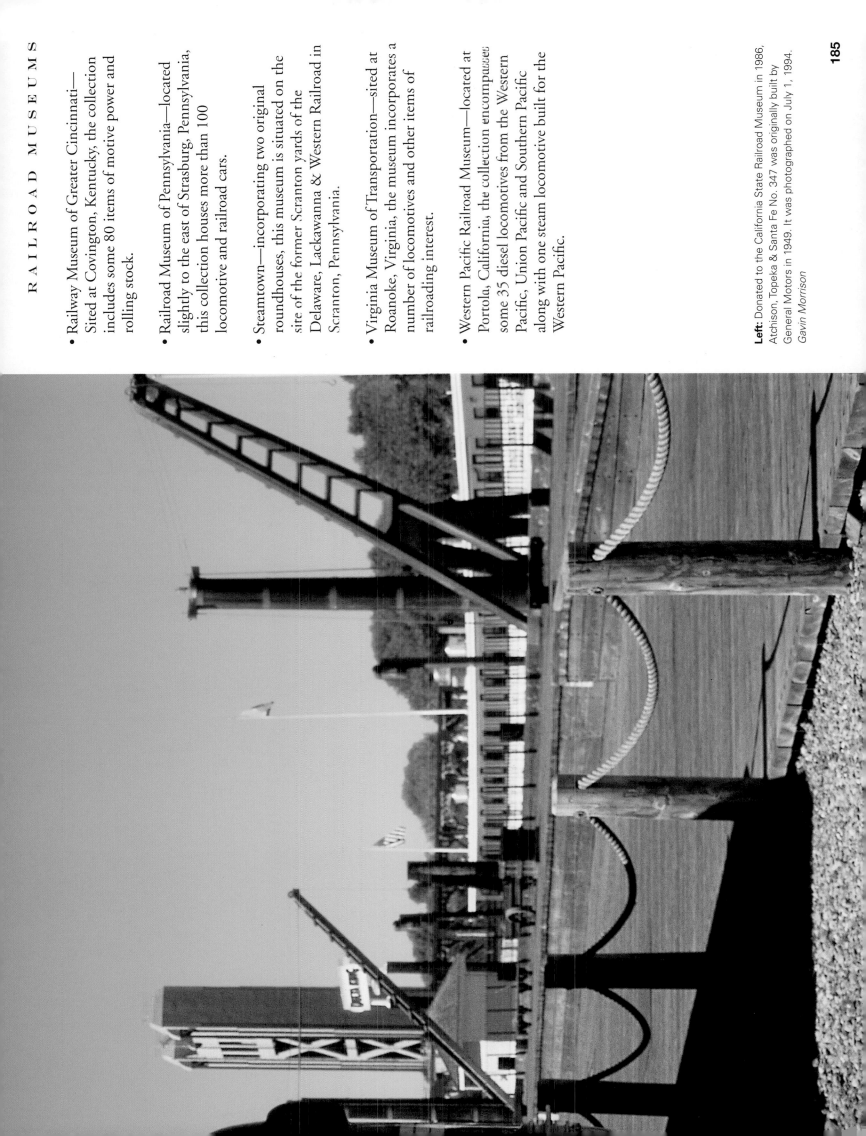

Left: Donated to the California State Railroad Museum in 1986, Atchison, Topeka & Santa Fe No. 347 was originally built by General Motors in 1949. It was photographed on July 1, 1994.
Gavin Morrison

185

Left and Right:
Manitou & Pikes Peak
No. 1 is a standard
gauge 0-4-2T
locomotive built by the
Baldwin Locomotive
Works to operate over
the M&PPR's cog
system. The locomotive
is now on display at the
Colorado State Railroad
Museum. *Both Brian
Solomon*

Left: Denver & Rio Grande No. 346 is one of a number of narrow gauge 2-8-0s on display at the Colorado State Railroad Museum. Although seen in steam here, this Baldwin-built Class C-19 locomotive is currently under restoration. *Brian Solomon*

Above: Colorado Railroad Museum. *Brian Solomon*

RAILROAD MUSEUMS

Far Left: The Railroad Museum of Pennsylvania is located close to Strasburg, Pennsylvania. *Brian Solomon*

Left: Ex-Nickel Plate Road No. 587—previously Lake Erie & Western Railroad 2-8-2 No. 5541—on display at the Indiana Transportation Museum. The locomotive, recorded here in 2000, is currently undergoing restoration. The locomotive was originally built in September 1918 by the Baldwin Locomotive Works. *Brian Solomon*

G R E A T   A M E R I C A N   S C E N I C   R A I L R O A D S